Witness to M~

Witness to Medjugorje
Healing & Conversion

I dedicate this book to the Holy Trinity, and to Our Lady Queen of Peace, and my utmost gratitude to those who have helped me in my hour of need. Also to those who are lost in faith, to those who are ill, to those who are the sufferers of Alcohol and Drug addiction, and to those who have lost their life's through suicide, and to their families they have left behind.

Vincent Duffy

Witnesses to Medjugorje

Published by Purple Heather Productions
Galway Ireland

Contents

Chapter One

The First Apparitions

It was a humid summers evening, when two teen-age friends, Ivanka Ivanković and Mirjana Dragićević were returning home from a stroll in the hills not far from Ivankas' home. On their descent Ivanka glanced towards one of the higher hills and to her disbelief, she saw a bright figure hovering in the sky. In shock and in an instant straight off she knew it was the Madonna. She turned to Mirjana and asked her to take a look at the Madonna up on the hill. Without looking, Mirjana waved her hand and said, "come on! You think the Madonna would appear to us!" she said, now frightened with the shocked expression on Ivanka's face.

On their way home, they met up with Milka Pav-lovic, aged twelve years old at the time. She asked the girls for their help in gathering their farm sheep and bringing them home. Without delay, they continued back up the hill where they had just been. It was approaching six-fifteen when they reached the foot of the hill where Ivanka had seen what she knew was the Madonna, Our Blessed Mother.

"Look, there she is." Mirjana and Milka said simultaneously, fearfully looking at the young woman who was dressed in grey holding something in Her hand which She seemed to be protecting. "She was a long way away," says Ivanka as she just made out the outline of her body, and could not see her face. Not knowing what the Madonna would really look like! But something inside them insisted that this was the Madonna. "We knew it was Her, but we were all confused, and just stood there looking at Her." Ivanka declares later to her family and friends, and like the others she was confused as to what to do. Together they all felt both joy and fearful as to why the Madonna chose to appear to them.

Then along came another teenage friend, Vicka Ivanković who was looking for Mirjana knowing she was by the hills. Mirjana, Ivanka and Milka waved at her eagerly for her to join them. When Vicka joined the girls, who seemed to be rather excited, Mirjana asked her to look at the Madonna, who had appeared up on the hill. "What do you mean the Madonna?" Vicka asked a little uneasy, thinking was Mirjana hallucinating or something to that effect. "What is the matter with you?" she added, not bothering to look, or even too afraid she might see the Blessed Virgin and what then. Nervously she kicked off her slippers she was wearing at the time, because they would most likely slip off, while she fearfully scampered down the narrow laneway towards the village, and home.

On her way there, she was still in doubt was Mirjana telling the truth. She met up with two other friends, Ivan Dravicevic who was sixteen-years old, and Ivan Ivankovic who was twenty. They were picking apples, and they asked her if she wanted some. Somewhat excited, Vicka refused the apples and excitedly told Ivan Dravicevic that Mirjana insists the Madonna had appeared to her, Ivanka and Milka up on the hill.

Now curious and abandoning the idea of going home, but too afraid to go back to the hill alone. She asked the two lads to accompany her to the hill, but Ivan was afraid. But in some way curiosity got the better of them, they decided to go to the hill to see for themselves. Within minutes they joined the others at the hill. Vicka hadn't seen the Madonna and asked Ivan did he see Her. Then turning to face him, she noticed he was gone, she saw Ivan running away. Then she asked Ivan Ivankovic did he see anything? He said he seen some sort of a figure, completely white. Milka said she sees the Madonna. Still looking, and then it began to rain a little, it was at this time Vicka seen the Madonna. Then the Madonna called them to come closer. Nervous and wondering should they get closer to Her. However none of them got any closer, since they were too afraid. Soon the Madonna diminished, and soon the teenagers made their way back down the hill. Mystified at what they had just witnessed, they decided to leave and go home barely even conversing to one another.

When they got to their houses, each of them gave an account of their experience to their family and friends. Though none of them believed what they had to say, and brushed it off, many scorned and laughed. Nonetheless, there was speculation among their families and friends, had the children been telling the truth. Some of them may believe, and others wondered could this be true.

"Her face was white, She was wearing a dark gown, and had dark hair. She was covering something She held in Her left arm." An excited Vicka disclosed to her family later that evening. Vicka's family laughed, suggesting it could have been some sort of a flying saucer, and did not believe her.

Mirjana explained to her family that there was an incredible light in the sky. "It was the Blessed Mother holding baby Jesus in Her arms. It was overwhelming," she explained. When asked by her family and friends, how did she know it was the Madonna? Mirjana replied, "My whole being knew without a doubt that this Lady of unexplainable beauty was defiantly the Mother of God. That is why I had such fear."

Next morning, everybody had to be up at first light to help harvest the leaves from the large tobacco plantation. For those who claim to have seen the Madonna on the hill and pondering in their minds all night long made it impossible for them to sleep.

Next evening at approximately six-pm, after harvesting the tobacco leaves, four of the teenagers, Ivanka Ivanković, Mirjana Dragićević, Vicka Ivanković and Ivan Dragićević, were compelled to go to the same hill where they had seen the Madonna the evening before. The hills were extremely over grown by wild prickly bushes, and uneven rocks, sharp and almost imposable to walk on. Still bewildered and confused as to why Our Lady had appeared to them. Marija Pavlović met up with ten-year-old Jakov Čolo who heard about the Madonna and for some reason was eager to see Her.

Additionally a number of curious adults and some young children tagged along in wonder as to what might happen. They then joined the four others on the foot of the hill. It was at this time that Ivanka suddenly turned and told the others to look at the Madonna floating in the sky. At that moment they heard the Blessed Mother calling them. She was beckoning at them to come closer.

The five teenagers, and young Jakov, instantly ran up Mount Podbrdo, leaving the others behind. They were suddenly thrown to their knees on the ragged edged rocks about seven-feet from Our Lady. Young Jakov was slammed to his knees, kneeling on prickly bushes, and after seeing this, they all thought he would be injured, but he was miraculously unscathed. Ivanka's mother had died two months previous and she asked the Blessed Mother about her. The Madonna told Ivanka that her mother is happy, and she is with Her, and that Ivanka should not worry.

Then Mirjana asked the Madonna, "that nobody will believe us that you have appeared to us. They will say that we are all crazy". But the Madonna just smiled. Mirjana along with the four teenagers stayed on the hill for ten to fifteen minutes before the other villagers had come up to join them. As they were about to leave, the Madonna seemed to be hovering in midair, and none of them teenagers did not know what to say to Her. Then the Blessed Mother said to them "Go in God's peace." The young teenager's heads were all turned in Her direction. Then She had left in the same direction as the evening before. Nobody who was there said a word, but everybody was in no doubt frightened.

"When we were on the hill praying with the Madonna on the second day, we prayed seven Our Fathers. We were praying because at this stage we did not know what else to do. We were crying a little and praying a little. Then the Madonna told us to pray seven Our Father's, ten Hail Mary's, Glory Be's, and the Credo." Mirjana discloses.

It was at this time the group of Medjugorje Visionaries was formed. From this moment on, those young visionaries' lives were never the same again. Their lives had been chained forever. Daily and monthly apparitions became an important feature in their lives. They were from a small village, not like young people who lived in large cities who are probably not as innocent, or even more street-wise. Those youths have never been anywhere away from home, school, or their families.

From then on, Our Lady made her messages known to the visionaries on a daily basis. Furthermore, through the visionaries, those special messages were announced to the whole world. Commencing from the 1st of March 1984, Our Lady began to give weekly messages on Thursdays to the parish community in Medjugorje, and through them to the rest of the world. The hill, in which Our Lady appeared, is now known as Apparition Hill. It was from that day onwards, the six visionaries had daily apparitions, together or separately, wherever they were at the time. But for some unknown reason, Milka Pavlović and Ivan Ivanković never saw the Blessed Mother ever again.

Our Lady said, She had chosen the parish of Medjugorje in a special way and wishes to lead it. I am guarding it in love and that She wants everyone to be

Hers. She asks us to accept Her and the messages She is giving us. Our Lady started to tell the visionaries the story of Her life. She said She will tell them in episodes of Her life. Our Lady has forbidden the visionaries to reveal Her life story to others until She has said everything. She has assigned to each of the visionaries the task to write Her biography and to disclose it to the world when She says so. Our Blessed Mother refers to us as Her children, because She is our Mother. She wants us to live by Her messages, by fasting, attending holy mass. She wants us to pray the rosary, and to encourage young children to attend holy mass and to make it the most important meaning in their lives.

On another visit the Madonna called on us to honour the wounds of Her Son Jesus Christ. She asked us to unite ourselves with Her prayers. Those who do not pray are lost. Those who do not pray have lost hope, those who pray little, are in great danger. It is through the power of prayer we receive God's graces. Pray, pray, pray in God's name and you shall not regret it. God has love for all humanity, for those with different believes. It is God's plan to bring those religions together to unite. God will give you gifts by which you will glorify Him until the end of your life on this earth.

In addition, Satan wants to frustrate Our Holy Mothers plans. He is working underhandedly against all parishes and especially the parish of Medjugorje. We are all to withstand the days of temptation. Our Lady doesn't want us to be afraid how Satan works, and not to be afraid of his temptations, because God is always watching over us. She also calls young people to be active in prayer. It is God's desire to convert the entire world. She also asked us to pray for our own conversion and the conversion of all sinners, and to look around us to see how sin has dominated our world. Pray, pray, pray, therefore, that Jesus conquers. She called on us to begin fasting with the heart, and not only because everyone else is fasting. She asks us to fast out of gratitude, and pray from the heart. She requests families to pray the rosary. Her heart is saddened for those who do not pray. She calls on us to read the Bible, and leave it in a visible place where it will always encourage us and others to read it.

We should always pray to God against evil. Pray to the Holy Spirit for enlightenment. She is Our Mother and She came to earth to teach us to listen out of love, to pray out of love and not be compelled by the fact that you are carrying the cross. It is Her Son who carried the cross for us, so we wouldn't have to. Without prayer there is no peace. Therefore I say to you, dear children, pray at the foot of the cross for peace, because I still need your prayers for the world to find peace. Thank you for having responding to My call.

Seeing as some of the things that Our Lord desired were fulfilled, as Our Lady said, from the 25th of January 1987 onwards She would give her monthly message to Marija on the 25th of each month. This has continued up until this present day. In addition, countless miracles have taken place in Medjugorje ever since the Blessed Virgin first appeared. Franciscan priest Janko Bubalo asked the young visionaries to describe the Blessed Mother's appearance. Each of them conveyed, She was between eighteen and twenty years old, and about five feet in height. She has a long, oval pale face, with rosy cheeks and black hair. Her eyes are blue with delicate eyelashes and very thin black eyebrows. She has a small nose and She has beautiful reddish thin lips. Her smile is more like some indescribable gentleness; it is visible as if somehow under her skin. Her simple dress is bluish-grey and falls freely all the way down to the little whitish cloud on which She is standing. She wears a white veil which covers Her head and shoulders, and on Her head, She wears a crown of twelve golden stars.

Father Janko also asked is Our Lady really as beautiful, as they have said? Their answer was that they really hadn't told him anything about that. Her beauty cannot be described. Somehow it is not our kind of beauty. It is something ethereal, something heavenly, something that we will only see in Paradise and then only to a certain degree.

Day after day, local people began to congregate in the parish of Medjugorje, to pray. Soon people came from other villages, town and cities in the region. Then word got around and other people recognized as pilgrims began to arrive from other nearby countries, and the entire world to pray for healing and conversion. Our Blessed Mother loves each and every one of us. Her desire is that we love one another, be at one with ourselves, our families, and God.

Chapter Two

The Visionaries

At the time of the first apparition, Vicka Ivanković was sixteen years old. She prays with Our Lady and talked to her. She has been given nine "secrets". She says the Blessed Virgin Mary told her to pray for the sick. Vicka has received a biography of Mary's life, which she has said will be published when the Blessed Virgin Mary tells her to do so.

Vicka continues to meet with pilgrims who visit Medjugorje and she has done so since Our Lady first appeared to her. She is known as the smiling visionary for the reason that her smile is filled with joy and love. Vicka says she once started to pray out of habit. Now she has turned completely to prayer. She has committed her life completely to God. She says she feels sorry for those who do not believe in God, because Our Lady wants no one to be lost

We can all help each other find the right way to God. It is up to the people to obey the messages and be converted. Great things are happening here in Medjugorje. Our Lady is among us. She wishes to attract everyone to Her Son Jesus Christ. That's the reason She has been appearing for so long and so often. Here on earth, everyone should feel the nearness and the Love of God the Father. It is a well-known documented medical fact, that Vicka had been plagued by a brain tumour for many years that caused severe headaches, coma state periods, nausea, etc. However, it was on the 25th of September 1988, the pain stopped. Vicka wrote about her healing, more or less six months previous to the healing. Father Janko Bubalo, along with two other priests who were all witnesses, received a sealed letter from Vicka. The letter was dated February 4th 1988 and they were told not to open the letter until September 25th of the same year. On that date when the letter was opened, Vicka immediately stopped having pains – just as it was stated in the letter. She had been miraculously healed. The president of the new commission who was assigned to study Medjugorje was present when the priests opened the letter. Also in attendance to witness this was Bishop Komarica who was the Bishop of the dioceses at the time.

Vicka's healing has to be of significance in helping establish the commission that the apparitions of the Blessed Mother are without doubt authentic. She and her husband and two children now live in Gruda, a small village a few kilometres north of Medjugorje.

Mirjana Dragićević-Soldo is the second oldest of all of the visionaries, a graduate from the University of Sarajevo where her family lived. She lives in Medjugorje, and is married to Mark Soldo and they have two daughters. She was the first to be told the ten secrets, which are now being entrusted gradually to the other visionaries. Her daily apparitions ceased on Christmas Day 1982, except for an annual visit from Our Lady on her birthday, March 18th. Mirjana has inner locutions on the second of each month, when Our Lady calls on her and all pilgrims to pray especially for unbelievers. It is Mirjana who will reveal the secrets to chosen priest, Father Petar Ljubicic, ten days before the events are due to occur. Her prayer assignment given by Our Lady is to pray for all unbelievers, and for those who have not come to know the love of God. She has entrusted her with the tenth secret. Since August 2nd 1987, on each second day of the month, she hears interiorly Our Lady's voice and prays with her for unbelievers.

Our Lady says that we cannot consider ourselves as true believers, if we do not see Jesus Christ in every single person we meet. Which means we are to respect each and every one of God's children. Our Lady also says we cannot save the non-believers, if not through our own prayer and example. She is asking us to give our utmost importance to prayer in their favour, because She has said that the worst things - such as war, divorce, abortion - come from people who do not believe. When you pray for them, you are also praying for yourselves, for your families and for the good of the world.

On June 24th, Ivanka Ivankovic-Elez was the first of the six visionaries who saw Our Lady. She was also the first to speak to Her, which happened on the following day, when Ivanka asked about her mother, for whom she was still greatly grieving. Our Lady responded by saying: "She is happy. She is with me, and that Ivanka should not worry. This had brought a sense of peace to Ivanka. She is the youngest of the girl visionaries. She was fifteen years old when the apparitions began. Her father was away working in Germany. It was in May 1981 when Ivanka's mother had died, a month before the apparitions began. Ivanka is described as pretty, with a serene but shy countenance. She was the second visionary, after Mirjana, to receive her tenth secret, signifying the end of her daily apparitions.

It was on May 6th 1985, Ivanka remained in ecstasy, while the apparition of the other three visionaries ended much sooner. They were astounded to see Ivanka's expression, realizing she was still seeing Our Lady. None of the visionaries had ever seen each other in ecstasy before. They all had watched in wonder, with all those present, until Ivanka's eyes drifted upward, signifying the end of her apparition. They all learned afterwards, that much to Ivanka's grief the next day would be sadly Our Lady's last daily apparition with her.

On May 7th 1985 Our Lady appeared with two angels in Ivanka's home. On that day, Our Lady told Ivanka that, no one in the world has had the grace which you, your brothers, and sisters have received. Our Lady was referring to the six visionaries. In this last apparition, Our Lady asked Ivanka if she had a wish. Ivanka truly replied, she would like to see her mother. This has been a request Our Lady has fulfilled for Ivanka on four separate occasions over the upcoming years. When Ivanka describes her favourite of these special visits, almost every time, her eyes fill with tears as she remembers the joy of that moment. "The third time I was so happy." she recalls. "I had completed a difficult assignment for the Blessed Mother. As a reward, She brought my mother to me. I had seen her two other times before, but the third time she came over to me, and embraced me and said, "Dearest Ivanka, I'm so proud of you!"

Ivanka had daily apparitions until May 7th 1985. On that day, confiding to her the tenth secret, Our Lady told her that for the rest of her life, she would have one yearly apparition, on June 25th, the anniversary of the apparitions. She lives with her family in Medjugorje. She is described as superficial, like a typical teenager, but more so than the other visionaries. Many years later, Ivanka herself admitted to having thought a great deal about fashion. Before the Blessed Mother began to appear to her, she thought of it all the time. As her prayer life grew, following fashion became boring and she lost interest.

Our Lady confirmed that Ivanka had matured in the spiritual life and that She was pleased by her efforts. Our Lady spoke these words to Ivanka the day of her final daily apparition. "With all your heart you have accepted the plans which my Son and I formulated, and you have accomplished everything." As She did with Mirjana and young Jakov, Our Lady gave to Ivanka a gift that would help to sustain her in this life after her daily apparitions ceased. She would be able to see Our Lady once a year, on the anniversary of the apparitions. Ivanka married Raiko Elez on December 28th 1986, which was the Feast of the Holy Family. Today, Ivanka and Raiko have three children. She was the first visionary to marry. There were those who expected all the visionaries to enter the religious life. And yet, Our Lady had made it clear to all of them, that they had freedom in deciding their own vocations. Now that all the visionaries have married, it would appear that the world is in need of witnesses to holy family life.

Ivan Dragicevic was sixteen-years-old when the apparitions began, and typical of a boy his age, he was not particularly religious. However, four days after the first apparitions, his mother found a rosary in his pants pocket. The apparitions have completely changed him. Ivan is one of the three visionaries who continue to have daily apparitions and he has been given nine secrets.

When speaking to pilgrims, Ivan shares the valuable information Our Lady has given him to help us find God. Ivan testifies to what he has been taught through the years by Our Lady without any anxiousness for people to believe what he says to be true. His attitude seems to be that each has the choice to believe or not to believe, and eventually one day all will know the truth. Ivan entered the priesthood seminary shortly after the apparitions began. He experienced great difficulties, not only academically, but emotionally and spiritually. During this time he spent in the "Little Seminary" in Dubrovnik Croatia, he suffered greatly, because of his relations with his colleagues and professors. He revealed that those in the seminary did not believe that he was seeing Our Lady. He had been constantly mocked and scorned. But despite the problems he was having at the seminary, Our Lady said to him, not to worry, that she will guide him through his life. Our Lady revealed his future to him. Now he is not afraid, because he knows She is guiding and protecting him. Our Lady has given instruction to Ivan about today's family and the youth and about those things that hurt and attack them. In one interview, Ivan stated that Our Lady has asked him to write a book, with Her help. This book will contain the disease of materialism, which She says is destroying the beauty of God's people and the world that He created. The book will be released as soon as the Blessed Mother gives him Her permission to do so.

Interestingly enough, Ivan married an American girl from Massachusetts, Laureen Murphy, who is a former Miss Massachusetts. Laureen has experienced conversion through Medjugorje, which eventually led to her meeting Ivan. Since their marriage, Ivan lives with his wife and children half of the year in Boston in the United States and the rest of the year in Medjugorje. Living within the culture of America has, no doubt, given Ivan a greater understanding of the evils of materialism than if he had remained within the region and culture in which he was born into.

Through the direction of Our Lady, Ivan, with Marija, started a prayer group of young people, who began meeting twice a week on Apparition Hill or Cross Mountain. During the prayer group meetings, Our Lady would normally appear to the visionaries, giving messages and instructions. She had asked them to offer their prayers for the fulfilment of her plans for the world. Tens of thousands, if not millions of pilgrims have joined this prayer group up on the mountains throughout the years. It is a great joy of Our Lady to see so many attend the prayer meeting, and come on pilgrimage. As in Her messages, She has often stated how happy She is to see everyone gathered in such large numbers. Those who come to Medjugorje while Ivan is there have the opportunity to be present at a prayer group meeting with Our Lady; an experience one remembers their entire life. Our Lady has said that every person in the world should belong to a prayer group. Ivan says that prayer groups are a protection from the triumph of Satan.

Jakov Colo is the youngest of the visionaries. He was only ten-years old when the apparitions began. He had daily apparitions from June 25th 1981 and up until September 12th 1988. It was on that day the Blessed Mother gave to him the tenth secret. Ever since, he has one yearly apparition on Christmas Day. When he was eight years old, his father abandoned the family, of which he was the only child. He had become an orphan at the age of twelve when his mother died. Since her death he lives with his uncle. It is Jakov who steals the heart when looking at old pictures of the visionaries in ecstasy from the first years of the apparitions. For many, it is he who convinced them the apparitions were real. As any normal ten-year-old boy would consider it impossible to have to endure three hours of prayer, on their knees, every single night, year after year, without any break in the routine. If the apparitions had been a trick or a lie, young Jakov would have broke long ago, yet, it is said that he was the most faithful in attendance to the evening prayer services in Medjugorje than any other visionary. Vicka, who was with Jakov more than the other visionaries, believed there was something really special about Jakov in his relationship with Our Lady, though it was a mystery even to her. When asked by her confessor why Our Lady chose little Jakov, Vicka said: "I can't say that I know the answer. But none of you really know the little guy! I always remember how the Virgin at the very start said: "The rest of you go, and let little Jakov remain with me." That is an unusual boy. Vicka make known.

Today, Jakov is a quiet and thoughtful man. He married at the age of twenty-two to Annalisa Barozzi, a young woman from Mantova Italy. They have three children and reside in Medjugorje. Though Jakov was given a great deal of suffering at an early age, especially with the loss of his mother, while coping with all the difficulties the apparitions had brought into his life. Nothing had prepared him for the announcement made to him by Our Lady on September 11th 1988. Jakov was in the United States at the time, in Miami, Florida, to speak at a conference. Our Lady appeared and told him that the next day would be his last apparition. It was the following day, September 12th, Our Lady confided to him his tenth secret. In his deep sorrow, Our Lady gave to him a gift, telling him that She would appear to him on Christmas Day every year until the end of his life. On that day, not only does he see Our Lady, but he receives the added joy of being in the presence of the Infant Jesus. Perhaps this is a special consolation given to Her youngest visionary because of all he had suffered in his young life. Even so, for Jakov who grew up with Our Lady, he certainly seen her as his Mother after he was left alone in the world. Long before his daily apparitions ended, when he was asked to speak of Heaven, he said, "If he thought of Heaven too much, he would certainly die of loneliness." What then must he suffer, to no longer having the comfort of Our Lady's apparitions each day?

In time, Jakov began to learn how to experience Our Lady in his heart without the joy of Her apparition. He had a realization in prayer, after several months of struggle that he was now like all other people, who must live their lives without seeing the Blessed Mother. This apparently has helped give him the strength to endure his suffering. Remembering the last words of Our Lady said to him that day, September 12th 1988, must also bring him much solace.

Marija Pavlovic-Lunetti grew up at the foot of Apparition hill, close to Vicka's house. She was sixteen when the apparitions began. Marija is deeply spiritual and prayerful, with a wonderful sense of humour. Marija has an immense ability to make a total stranger feel as though they are really long lost friends. These attributes are just as much a part of Marija's character as the prayerfulness and serenity that have always been told about her.

Marija's sincerity and deep desire is for all to fall in love with Our Lady. On March 1st 1984, Our Lady began giving, every Thursday evening, a weekly message for the parish of Medjugorje. It was Marija through whom Our Lady entrusted these messages for the parish. Through these messages, Our Lady desired to spiritually form the parish because of the special role it would play in helping to bring conversion to all the people who would come to Medjugorje from all over the world. In time, this weekly message evolved into the monthly message for the world, given on the 25th of each month.

It was on January 25th 1987, when the first monthly message was given from Our Lady. Marija is the only visionary who receives this message. It stays within her memory only until she writes it down. After it is written, she no longer can repeat the message word for word. Marija has said that Satan causes "great confusion" in her life on the 25th of each month. He strikes back at the one who delivers Our Lady's healing words to a sick and destructive world. This gives evidence that Our Lady's words, each month are causing havoc to Satan's evil designs for the world. As Our Lady began to initiate the parish of Medjugorje into an intense spiritual life through the young visionaries, Marija began to feel the pull to the religious life. She, with Ivan, under the direction of Our Lady, began a prayer group of young people, and through the years Our Lady led them towards a profound love of Jesus and the Holy Mass.

It was the decision of Marija to enter a religious order, but as she began to look at possible orders to join. She began to realize that to accept the Rule of the orders meant, she would lose the freedom to openly witness to the apparitions and spread Our Lady's messages. In her heart, there was no question of what her responsibility was in regards to being a chosen witness of the apparitions in Medjugorje. She could not join a religious order if it meant having to stop spreading the messages of Our Lady.

Also, as Our Lady's plan became clearer to the visionaries, they began to understand that vocations to the religious life were best filled by those who were raised in holy families. With holy families there will never be a lack of good and plentiful vocations.

With Our Lady's guidance, it was at that point that Marija became open to marriage for the first time. She eventually did marry a young man from Milano Italy, who had been a good friend of hers for approximately five years. Their wedding took place on September 8th 1993. They live in Monza Italy, and are often in Medjugorje, especially during the summer months. Marija and Paolo have four young sons, all whom were given Marija as their middle name: Michele Marija, Francesco Marija, Marco Marija, and Giovanni Marija. It is interesting that Marija ended up marrying an Italian man. As one of the more incredible gifts Our Lady gave to her early in the apparitions was, in an instant, the ability to understand and fluently speak native Italian. She received it in an apparition on her birthday. Marija entered the apparition without being able to speak fluent Italian, Our Lady gave Her the gift of the language, and Marija left the apparition speaking it better than one who has studied to learn to speak it as a language. Now it is like a native language for her.

Another great grace Our Lady has bestowed upon the world through Marija, is the Special Blessing. It is a blessing of conversion that once we receive it, helps to lead us towards conversion our entire life. Our Lady once said that conversion is a process that ends only after we die. The gift of this blessing is that we can pass the blessing on to others, and it will help them in the same way it helps those who have already received it. No other visionary was given knowledge of the Special Blessing. Only Marija has details concerning it, just as only Mirjana and Vicka were given the special prayers for non-believers. This Special Blessing helps Our Lady reach hearts that in many ways are unreachable. And through an act of love from one of Her children who is moved to grant Her blessing upon them, it is enough to open a heart to grace. Marija said, Our Lady wants the Special Blessing to be used. She wants it to change our mentality that we, as laity, should understand we are to bless others. She wants us to do this through Her Special Blessing. Of all of Marija's gifts, one who is close to her believes the gift that Our Lady has given her above all others is the gift of love.

Our Lady has given Her love specifically five different times in known messages, as of July 2009, and three of these five times have occurred at Caritas in Alabama. The first time Our Lady gave Her love at Caritas was in the bedroom of the Apparitions before the Community began. During the apparition, the host family and those present felt love intensely. After the apparition, Marija relayed Our Lady's message: "Dear children, I give you my love, so you give it to others." A reporter said that Marija's voice was beautiful, gentle, full of love and intensity when she spoke about the apparition just after Our Lady left. All felt Our Lady's presence and sensed that She was happy in a special way. Those gathered really felt Our Lady gave them Her love. Love filled the room so much that one witness said he felt as though love permeated even the walls of the bedroom. The other two times, also were in the bedroom, in which Our Lady gave a message saying, She was giving Her love. Marija seems to be an extension of Our Lady's love to the world. Marija gave insight to this when Father Slavko, a Medugorje priest who asked her to choose the most beautiful and the most difficult of all messages. She told him that once she had asked Our Lady if She had something concrete to give her. Our Lady answered, "Yes, I give you my love, so that you give it to others."

Marija then said to Father Slavko. "To experience the beauty of Our Lady's love, and to know that it is that love which gives itself to you. It is the most beautiful thing in life. But, when I try to love others and try to give that love to them, then that is difficult. I often feel shame for my insufficiencies to love in the light of Our Lady's all encompassing motherly love."

Then he asked her. "What can be done?"

Marija responded, "I pray every day that I may be all the more open to this love of Our Lady, and that I may be able to pass it onto every person. I pray for others that they may be able to feel this love and in turn give it to others. We are so far from loving one another and this is a sign that we are also far from God's love. And the closer we are to God's love, the easier we will be able to live that love and bear witness to others."

Chapter Three

Our Lady's Secrets

There is very little known about the ten secrets Our Lady has given to the six visionaries. The visionaries can share very little information about the secrets. She has told the six visionaries that the third secret will be a sign placed on Apparition hill permanent, indestructible, beautiful and will appear spontaneously. The sign will appear on the mountain in such a way that unbelievers won't have words to say what it is. The sign will be something that has never been on the earth before.

All six visionaries know what the sign will be. They have said that it will be a beautiful, indestructible, permanent sign for all mankind to see forever. Our Lady's plan is, to correct man's conscience and save the world. When Mirjana received all ten secrets, she was not confident that she would be able to remember all the dates and details of each secret. Our Lady literally gave her a parchment during an apparition. This parchment is made of a material not found here on earth, with all the secrets written on it, as well as the day and date each of them will occur.

The Blessed Mother told Mirjana that she was to choose a priest to reveal the secrets to the world. Mirjana chose Father Petar Ljubicic and he has accepted this responsibility. Three of the six visionaries have all ten secrets and no longer see Our Lady on a daily basis. The following is just a brief summary of the most important points about the ten secrets. These points are taken from the more detailed information in this section about the ten secrets. - Our Lady is giving ten secrets to the Medjugorje visionaries that will bring worldwide conversion to the world.

God is giving so much time for these apparitions, so that all may come to conversion. - Three of the visionaries, Mirjana, Ivanka, and Jakov have all ten secrets and no longer see Our Lady on a daily bases. - Marija, Vicka, and Ivan have nine secrets. - Part of the seventh secret has been mitigated through prayer and fasting. - Mirjana is the visionary whom Our Lady gave the responsibility to reveal the secrets. - Father Petar Ljubicic is the priest chosen by Mirjana to reveal the secrets to the world. - Father Petar agrees to read each secret ten days before it occurs. He will fast for seven days. Three days before the secret happens, he will announce them to the world, and then the secrets will happen.

During the time of the ten secrets, one of the visionaries will still have daily apparitions. - Not all the secrets are the same for all the visionaries. Some of Ivan and Vicka's secrets are personal ones for them. And lastly, we know that the ninth and tenth secrets are chastisements for the sins of the world.

From the start, the communist police opposed the visionaries claims that the Madonna was appearing to them on the hill. They arrested the six Visionaries along with, Franciscan monks Father Jozo Zovko who favoured the six visionaries. Father Jozo was beaten and sent to prison. Then he was put before a firing-squad for

his belief and supporting of the visionaries. He was prepared to die rather than go against his faith that the
Madonna was appearing on the hill. But instead of plac-
ing live ammunition in the soldier's rifles, the police re-
placed them with blanks, leaving the faithful priest to
live another day.

The Yugoslav secret police from Sarajevo came to
investigate the visionaries. Their mission was to threaten
and scare the people congregating in Medjugorje. They
regularly patrolled the village and hills, threatening the
devoted villagers, and pilgrims with their firearms.

It is said that the Bishop of Mostar, Monsignor
Pavao Žanić, who initially was open to the possibility
that a paranormal occurrence was taking place. He celebrated Mass in Medjugorje and defended the young visionaries. But when he read reports presented to him by
the secret police, his views were altered and he soon opposed the visionaries' claim. Was he pressured into becoming an unbeliever, so he wouldn't face prison like
Father Jozo?

It has become obvious that Monsignor Pavao Žanić's
mind was changed by the series of documents which
was put together by the Yugoslav Secret Police. Those
documents were circulating at at time, and a copy was
also sent to the Vatican. Is it likely that the Monsignor's
mind was changed, because he felt that he needed to go
along with the communist police out of fear? And was
also his successor, the current pastor of Mostar, Ratko
Peric, following the same opinion, opposing the visionaries without even meeting them? Is this the reason the

Vatican has not approved the Visionaries claims? Or is it that the Vatican and our past Pope's are being loyal to those documents that were early reports by the communist police?

How are we sure the visionaries aren't making these apparitions up? There have been three extensive scientific studies done on the visionaries since the apparitions began in Medjugorje, by the best scientists in the world. The most recent of which was in 1998. All drew the same conclusion, which are that the visionaries are healthy mentally and physically. They are not hallucinating, are not lying, and are definitely experiencing something that is beyond our scientific understanding that is unexplainable. Most likely they are being visit by Our Blessed Mother, sent to earth by God. It is also interesting to note that during the experiments, one of the things being monitored was brain activity. Most of us are able to use around ten-percent of our brain during normal activities. It is fascinating to note that at the moment when Our Lady appears, the visionaries brain activity jumps to one-hundred percent, and stays at this level until Our Lady leaves.

Doctor Michael W. Petrides has done extensive study of the brains' laterality, activity, abilities and visual perception research at the Institute of Living. He has fundamental doctoral training in clinical psychology at Saint Louis University. He currently directs the Psychiatric Outpatient Clinic's mental health services for Catholic Charities in the Diocese of Norwich, Connecticut. It was in 1993, when he carried out a scientific study on the six visionaries of Medjugorje. His report on the six visionaries is the first in history to be methodically investigated by science.

Professor Henri Joyeaux headed a team from the University of Montpellier, France. Dr. Frigerio and colleagues from Italy did further investigations. The regularity of the apparitions has made for consistent and extremely reliable findings. Five alleged visionaries tested were found to simultaneously look at precisely the same spot. Even though no reference point was visible, within one-fifth of a second of each other when the Blessed Virgin Mary allegedly appears. Such synchronization can only be explained by some external "object" holding their gaze - but nobody else around them could see anything.

During the same one-fifth of a second, there are simultaneous kneeling and the cessation of eye movements. There is no eye movement during the entire apparition. There is also the simultaneous raising of their heads and gazing upwards while remaining fixated on a spot moving upwards when the apparition is finishing.

In his Christmas address 2015, His Eminence, Cardinal Vinko Puljic, Archbishop of Vrhbosna, Sarajevo, said, that Medjugorje is a parish which is under the jurisdiction of the local Bishop of Mostar. It is the Franciscans, who organise its daily duties. Unless, otherwise decided, people have the right to come to God to pray and to do penance.

Prayer to Holy Spirit

Holy Spirit, I Offer Myself, Soul and Body to You, Eternal Spirit of God. I Adore the Brightness of Your Purity, the Unerring Keenness of Your justice, and the Might of Your Love. You are the Strength and Light of My Soul. In You I Live and Move. I Desire Never to Grieve You by Unfaithfulness to Grace and I Pray with all my Heart to be kept from the Smallest Sin against You.

Mercifully Guard my Every Thought and Grant that I may Always Watch for Your Light and Listen to Your Voice and Follow Your gracious Inspirations. I Cling to You and Give Myself to You and Ask You, by Your Compassion, to Watch over me in my Weakness. Holding the Pierced Feet of Jesus and Looking at His Five Wounds and Trusting in His Precious Blood and Adoring His opened Side and Stricken Heart, I Implore You, Adorable Spirit, Helper of my Infirmity, so to Keep me in Your Grace that I may Never Sin against You. Give me Grace, O Holy Ghost, Spirit of the Father and the Son, to say to You Always and Everywhere, "Speak, Lord, for Your servant Heart." Amen.

Chapter Four

Growing up in Ireland & Some...

It was in the late fifties when I was born; and became the eighth child of twelve children in our family. My father was a modest farmer, farming an average of forty-five acres of prime, fertile, and grazing land. We had many farm animals, for instance, like milking cows, pigs, turkeys, chickens and hens. We had some fantastic times back then. Many times my brothers, sisters and I playing football in the back yard along with hide and go seek in the hay barns. We would close our eyes and give the younger ones five minutes to hide in a secret place. Sometimes we would find them hiding in the apple chest up in one of the lofts in the storage barns. There were terrifying moments when one of us would have no choice but to reveal our hiding place. As a barn mouse or even a large rat would appear from beneath old canvas sacks, and run right by you. The strident screams were enough to give your hiding place away.

At one stage, I had found a great hiding place right in the middle of the backyard, where nobody would even contemplate to search. I had tunneled an opening underneath one of the straw stacks and hid inside. There was no way my brothers would find me there. I could hear them mooch about in the nearby sheds, sometimes they would come so close to me I could almost touch their boots. Restraining the giggles was the difficult part. Another great hiding place was high up on the canopy of the pine trees. This was my favorite hiding place of all, as my brothers would search for me, I would call out. They would rush into the woods; but I was in the perfect hiding place. It was impossible to find me where I hid among the dense branches, and soon they gave up.

There were times I loved to sit up on that canopy and watch the world go by. I enjoyed favorable moments watching our neighbours going about their daily business, plowing the fields, and rezoning for the springtime crops. From high up on the canopy, I would be mystified, as I would watch the darkened soil plowed field become green from emerging potato foliage, turnips, and sugar beet. What's more, to watch the tillage fields become a beautiful shade of light yellow with oats and barley, was a wonderful sight. Still, to see my neighbours harvest the crops in nearby fields in the autumn, was a magnificent experience, and to hear the farm machinery echo in the distance.

I would often watch wild birds build their nests in nearby trees, and weeks later could hear the newborn chicks chirping in their nests. Once there was a Magpie's nest right next to me on top of one of the trees. I would sit there in the spring evenings after school and watch the parent Magpie's feed their chicks worms and insects they would hit upon rummaging about in the animal farm manure. There were times when the adult Magpie's would arrive with chunks of my mum's homemade bread she would use as feed for the chickens, geese and turkeys. As far back as I can remember, I wasn't too enthusiastic to work the land. Nevertheless, having farm chores was all part of growing up on a farm. Summertime was special in the early seventies, with bright skies and up to twenty-seven degrees heat. My brothers and sisters had a lot of great fun with some of the farm animals, like riding on the donkey's back. The large pigs would give us one by one a fast ride across the garden, stopping in their tracks and topple us head over heels, most likely on top of a pile of pig pooh. We had lots of laughter and teased one another as brothers and sisters do in a friendly manner. Equally, we enjoyed watching TV together. Our living room resembled a miniature cinema, especially when the All Ireland Football final was broadcasted live. Occasionally lots of our neighbours would stop by to watch the matinee on Sunday afternoons.

At primary school, we were taught by the Sisters of Charity, the nuns resided in the Convent in close proximity to the school. Attending national school was a special time for me. I had the chance to make friends and learn how to read and write, which was geography, history, and cooking were my favorite subjects. It was magic attending school in those early years. In fact, I came first in my class many times for writing short stories and cooking. As a result, one of the nuns gave me great encouragement to train as a Chef when I'd leave school. She had a point, because at this stage I enjoyed cooking and often helped my mum cook for our family and sometimes extended family members when they would come to visit. To add, there were some not so favourable moments, like playing a game of hurling was not in my curriculum. Hurling was widespread in our area. One blustery afternoon while I was a goalie for our class hurling team and as the ball was hurled towards me, and not knowing what I was supposed to do. In a panic, I whacked the ball into my own goal, scoring a goal for the opposite team. There was such laughter by the remainder of the class, it riled up our trainer Sister Katherine. She raced towards me in a fierce bluster, bellowing her referee whistle and brandishing her flag. She pinched my ear, and hauled me to the sideline. She never knew the favour she did for me that day, taking me off the school team. In fact from then on, I never held a hurly in my hand ever again.

Unfortunately, one evening after school while I was in one of our barns repairing a puncture on my bicycle, I was approached by a man six-years my senior, and twice my size. He was known to be violent and aggressive. I saw him fight many times with local guys, which scared me. Little did I know that what was about to happen would change my life forever. With one hand he gagged my mouth, and manhandled me to the floor. He cautioned me not to call out or he would kill me. Subsequently he forced himself on me, and buggered me, in which this horrific act was horribly painful. Before he left the barn, once again he threatened to kill me, if I told anybody about what just happened. I was nine-years of age. This was a horrible experience. Previous to this, I had never known anything about this sort of stuff.

Next evening, he dragged me into one of the barns, and repeated the same horrible act, threatening me afterwards. I was scared to tell my parents, because of his threats and his brutality. Another time when I entered one of the barns to fetch my bicycle, there he was standing silently in the dark, behind the barn door. With his piercing eyes peering towards me, almost like the stare of a crazed beast. My immediate reaction was to run before he had the chance to get his hands on me, because I knew what was about to happen. The stare in his eyes scared me and said it all, as he grabbed me and bolted the barn door from inside.

This repellent practice had been performed on my person many times for many years after. I became terrified of this guy's threats that he would kill me, if I told anybody about what he was doing to me. I felt dirty inside, and all the scrubbing in the world, would never wash the dirty feeling away. I became so intimidated and frightened, I began wetting the bed, and terrified of older men.

Before this horrific ordeal, when older guys would stop by, we'd have fun playing football and sometimes going to the nearby river to fish. One or two of them had even repaired my bicycle in the past. All this had changed drastically, after what this evil person had done to me. When I would hear a car or tractor enter our yard, I would run in doors, usually to my bedroom and peep through the drapes until they left. I had developed a deep fear for older men, because the guy who was doing all this sexual stuff to me, had said most men did this sort of thing. Nevertheless, when I asked who else does this, his reply was, "it is their secret, they do not tell anybody". When I threatened to tell my parents, he would beat me repeatedly, and threaten to kill me, saying, nobody would believe me. The beatings became more frequent when I refused to meet his request. Sometimes I managed to run away from him, but this was short lived.

Once I managed to run away from him, and threatened to tell my parents on him. However, he was much faster than I, he grabbed me and tried to suffocate me by blocking my airways with his hand. Another time when I threatened to tell one of my older sisters what he was doing to me, he threw a rock at me and put a deep wound on the left side of my head where I received a couple of stitches. I became so scared of this person; I had no choice but to meet his desires. I felt a great burden inflicted upon me, and I was still only twelve years old. I knew sexual stuff that a boy at my age was not supposed to know. Nightmares became a regular occurrence, and I was inflected with deep negative feelings of shame, guilt and remorse. I felt dirty and the grief of emptiness in my heart; it was some sort of low feeling that I could never comprehend. I felt a deep sadness inside me that this person had this great hold over me, in which suicide became a way out. I refused to do any sort of work on the farm when he was about, in which this angered my father. I became afraid to enter the barns, in case he was lurking about waiting for me to enter. I became afraid of most people, and would shy away if they were about to approach me.

There was such violence inflicted upon me and vicious attacks, I ate very little, and did not respond very well in school. Sleep deprivation meant falling asleep in class was a regular occurrence. I was withdrawn and had very little attentiveness. Studying at school became a burden. The ability to maintain or learn anything became almost unbearable, because anything I read, or what the teachers were teaching would not stay in my head. I began to suffer from memory lapse, only remember part of what I was been taught. I enjoyed writing; I guess this helped me to maintain my sanity, writing down different events that would occur at home and at school.

The head teacher in the school recommended to my parents, I attend another school in the city, for so-called slow learners. To which I refused to go. All areas of my life had become affected; my relationship with the rest of my family had changed. I became very angry. The only place I felt safe from this abusive person, was when I was in the kitchen cooking with my mother and doing household chores.

My relationship with my father started to deteriorate because of my refusal to work on the farm. I developed a tendency to get riled up when I was asked to do work on the farm. It was at this point my father and I by no means saw eye to eye over the land. We both rebelled against one another. He would regularly beat me with a stick or with the palm of his hand to get me to do farm chores. What seemed like the thousandth time, he'd yell in a rage, that I would never have a day's luck, ever, because of the way I had rebelled against him. This was the most horrific time in my life. "If you do not respect your father, you cannot respect yourself", he'd yell at me.

I had lost honor for him because of the way he fought and rejected me. Somehow, he would never admit his wrongdoing. I was blamed for everything that went wrong in the farm. Sometimes, he would yell, "it was my entire fault". *How was I such a bad child*? Why did he hate me so much? This made me feel an outcast in the family. I felt I had nothing in common with my parents or brothers and sisters to any further extent. The loneliness was soul destroying. If any items inside the house or farmyard were broken or gone missing, it seemed almost every time, I would get the blame. I felt victimized, and was made feel like an escape-goat for the entire family, to cast blame on me for some unknown reason or other.

Once I enraged one of my brothers because I sat on his chair, while he went to the kitchen. He returned with a kitchen knife, and stabbed me in the back of my left wrist. Receiving a large gash straight to the bone, my immediate reaction was to cover it with my right hand and close the gash. Then taking to the bed where I lay there through the night awake so the wound would knit together.

My first drink and smoke was a bottle of Guinness and one on my father's woodbines. I had found them behind the couch in the living room, after a family gathering. Taking to the garden sipping the bottle and having a couple of drags from the woodbine, made me dizzy and my legs felt like jelly. I guess this experience wasn't too much of a buzz, figuring this wouldn't be my last. At home, we always prepared our own butter. This was primarily a task for me. I would load the cream into the churn container, and twist the handle to rotate the churn. Sometimes I would place my finger on to the moving gears, and watch my finger become black with the grease. However, this was a stupid move. My finger had been trapped between the gears, and had crushed it badly. Then my father hollered that I did this in purpose, so I could get out of churning the butter. How wrong he was, because I truly looked forward to watching the cream break and turn to form larger fat globules and eventually forming butter.

Another painful incident occurred. It was one freezing blistery autumn evening after school. My father and brothers were loading sugar beet into the tractor-trailer. By accident, I had pierced my boot with the prong of the beet fork and it went straight through one of my toes on my left foot. The weird thing was that my father yelled at me, that I did this in purpose, to get out of loading the sugar beet. After a while, the bleeding stopped, and two-hours later and chilly to the bone, we headed home. My mum dipped my toe in antiseptic, and wrapped a piece of cloth around my foot, before I was sent to my bed.

Going through life without love from my father wasn't easy, it plagued my thoughts and I could not comprehend why my life was so laborious. Years later while in therapy, I discovered at the tender age of twelve or thirteen, I became vulnerable, insecure, inferior and sensitive. Somehow, developing a way to hide my true feelings from others. Never showing others that my feelings were hurt, why I did this I will never know.

I always kept my feelings hidden, and managed not to show hurt on my facial expression. Developing a false laugh, to blanket over my negative feelings. Maybe if I had shown my hurts people would not have hurt me so much. To cover over those negative feelings I would sing a lot. In my heart, I wanted to sing professionally. At school I was told by my teacher, I had a great singing voice.

It was the mid-seventies, and the Glam Rock era was now in full swing, with the most outrageous clothes, fashionable trendy hairstyles, and platform boots. My favourite singers were Alvin stardust, Marc Boland & T Rex, David Bowie, and Gary Glitter. At the time it seemed Gary Glitter was my God. How wrong I was. Somehow my dream was short lived, as I was being mocked and discouraged by a family member to be a singer. He would poke remarks, saying that I could not sing. I was too ugly to be a singer. People would laugh at me if I came out on the stage with my large ears, small eyes, and long nose covered in pimples. This hit below the belt, I became so vulnerable I believed such discourteous remarks about my person. This was a bitter pill to swallow, to think that I was so ugly; I could never be a professional singer. What hurt the most, was years later the person who had said this hurtful stuff about my looks. At social outings, he himself would go on the stage to sing. It was obvious he played the hierarchy to break me down, so he could have the glory. What a sick person to do this to another, just to feed his own ego. When I'd hark back on how wrongly I had been treated,

I wanted out. At the age of fourteen, I made my way to a nearby river with a rope, taken from one of the barns. Standing on the foot-bridge with the rope secured to a rock, and ready to jump. A voice in my head told that this would destroy my mother, whom I loved dearly.

As tears well, guilt and remorse had overpowered my thoughts. *"Was this a selfish act?"* So I decided to refrain from taking my own life. Lucky for me, and not before time, the ill minded person who was abusing me, left the village and went to work abroad. By the time I was sixteen, all I saw in the mirror was an incensed ugly guy staring back at me. This made me very ashamed of who I was, and made me very angry towards myself and the vulgar people who planted those negative thoughts in my head. I could not wait for the time to come, until I'd leave home and get away from those people. My father wanted me out of the house because of the constant arguments. My mother and family seemed to take his side. On the other hand, she worried about my aggression and because I was not learning in school. She decided to take me to a faith healer who visited a nearby town. I have very little memory about this experience, only he left his hands on my shoulder and muttered a couple of words.

There was a time I would share personal issues with my mother, that was going on in my life. You think you could trust your mother? Well years later, it was revealed to me that she was revealing to other members of my family and close relatives what I had conveyed to her. This broke my trust, not only with my mother, but for almost every other person who had entered my life from then on. Sometimes it was almost impossible to fit in with other people. I began to fit into their personality, rather than be myself.

Chapter Five

Accidents & Misfortune

When I became of age to go to the pubs, I felt very shy, introverted, and inhibited to other people. Entering a crowded place became the scariest thing on earth. Soon I discovered, by having a couple of drinks before entering the crowed pubs or clubs, the fear would leave me. Feeling free of those negative feelings, I had confidence and became an extrovert when I drank.

Preferably, I did not smoker, but most times I would drink more alcohol than my body could handle. Somehow my accident-prone life continued. I came off my motorcycle a couple of times. Once my Honda skidded out of control and crashed into a marshy ditch and into a bog swamp. I was lucky I was able to get out of the freezing water to safety. Unfortunately, weeks later a friend came off his motorcycle in the exact same area. He went into the bog swamp and tragically drowned. Woefully, it seemed I had not learnt my lesson. There was another occasion after leaving the pub with my girlfriend. We came off the motorcycle, and slid along the oily-slippery road. As a result, she had a swollen knee and I had a large gash to my right arm. Regrettably, my motorcycle was pretty bashed up too, after it crashed into a fence. In addition, she suggested we part our ways from then on. Having survived these accidents, I decided to trade my motorcycle for a motor car; it was navy blue Austin Mini, knowing cars are much safer than motorcycles. One day while heading back to the garage where I had purchased the car to have its breaks adjusted. Hadn't one of the rear wheels somehow detached itself and flew right past us! My brother, who was a nervous passenger, had passed comment as to where the speeding wheel came from. Within an instant, you could hear the screeching sound of metal scrape along the tar macadam. Whilst my brother was hollering for his life, I on the other hand, tried helplessly to control the car from crashing into an oncoming articulated truck. It seemed the car had taken on a life of its own, swerving from one side of the road to the other. Somehow, I managed to get it under control and onto the ditch and bring it to a safe halt. My brother reassured me that this was the first and last time he was ever going to travel as a passenger while I was the driver.

Quickly I reminded him of the time he turned over my father's Mk2 Cortina, with five passengers on board. Not alone that, I was binned down by the other passengers; my face was pressed against the glass of the back door as the car which seemed forever, slid along the road. You could only cringe at the consequences of what would happen to my face it the glass had somehow smashed. Unlucky for me there were a couple of other minor accidents, like crashing my car into walls and ditches coming home from pubs and nightclubs. It seemed I had become reckless with my life, living on the edge, and on a wing and a prayer. Failing to hold down a full time job resulted in losing flats, and sleeping out a couple of times underneath the stars.

The summer nights were not so bad. The winter's nights were a completely different story, waking up in an alleyway after a couple of hours barely able to move from the chills. Sleeping in a car or van wasn't so bad, at least I was in from the harsh weather. Still, it was a horrible existence, especially when you thought of everybody else tucked up in his or her warm beds.

Having no fixed abode was a daunting experience. It is very easy to judge homeless people who live in those circumstances. So many people judge the homeless; nobody knows what their lives were like before they became homeless. Most of those unfortunate people have suffered some sort of abuse as children, which lead to depression and failure. People should try and live in a homeless person's shoes, before passing judgment. Thank God most of the time I could work and afford a flat in the city.

It seems most of us are moulded at a very early age to choose a profession, and remain in that particular job or vocation until retirement age like doctors, teachers, nurses and bankers etc. I always struggled with what I wanted to do with my life. Of course at a very early age, being a lead singer in a band looked very attractive to me at the age of fourteen or fifteen, but that was short lived. By the time I reached eighteen, I had over twenty positions of employment behind me. One of them was serving my time in a hotel as a trainee chef. This did not work out, so I decided to serve my time in a garage as an apprentice spray mechanic. Other odd jobs were gardening, shop assistants, and labouring in a couple of building sites. None of which I carried through. I encountered a job as a helper on a wholesale delivery truck, which encouraged me to take driving lesions for a heavy goods vehicle license.

I met a beautiful girl and fell in love. We had some great times, and some not so great times. One evening after having a couple of drinks with a friend, I was run over by a passing motorist as I dashed across the street, to avoid getting wet as it rained heavily. It turned out the driver of the car was a priest. I was informed afterwards the priest had anointed me as I lay unconscious on the pavement. I was taken to the general hospital, where there was a fracture to my scull, to my shinbone on my left leg, and a broken wrist. Guess it was my own fault because my judgment was impaired by alcohol.

There were many times my girlfriends pleaded with me not to drink so much, and try to control my temper. It seemed when somebody got my back up or anything would go wrong, I had only one way of reacting to my feelings, I would fly off the handle in a rage. If the car broke down, or if somebody criticized me, it seemed I could not handle it very well. I became so reckless, it frightened her. Driving while under the influence became a regular occurrence. I guess she had enough after I received a punch to the face after a quarrel with a guy in a nightclub, over something stupid. Again, I was hospitalized, with a split tongue and a deep gash to my lip.

I received nine stitches to my tongue, and six to my upper lip. It took a full two weeks before I could chew my food. I could only drink liquids, even this was challenging. This took its toll on our relationship. She had enough. It was heartbreaking when she travelled abroad on holidays and took up residence there; we never made contact with one another after that. I was saddened by this, since my hopes were we would marry one day.

All the same, life goes on, and eventually I obtained a full driver's license, after repeating the driving test three times. I then acquired a job driving a delivery truck. Nevertheless, I still carried on being self-destructive, with many other visits to the A&E over cuts and bruises. Never drinking while driving the truck, I might add. An additional mishap happened while I was weight training; a twenty-kilo dumbbell came unattached from the weight-training bar and crushed one of my toes. I spent up to three-weeks on crutches. On another occasion, I got a fractured nose from a nightclub door that was slammed on my face, by accident. I had also received numerous black eyes from fights and falls.

It was two days before Christmas, 1981, when I slipped in a public house breaking up a fight. A twenty-stone man, who was a friend of my brothers slipped and fell onto the inside of my knee and bent it like a piece of cardboard. Again, I was hospitalized with torn ligaments, damaged cartilage and a fractured kneecap, all to my left knee.

It was embarrassing in the hospital ward, when I'd hear the squeaking sound of a hospital trolley approach with my files. Most doctors or nurses would carry their patient's files under their arm. No, not mine, there were so many files, the nurse had to wheel them to the ward by trolley. The other patients often passed comments, how young I was to have so many hospital records.

Amongst all this madness, I then met a woman who was the total opposite to me. Who lived a very serene life, none drinker, was kind and rather good looking. I was attracted to her lifestyle, but I knew deep down I was not in love with her. My heart was with the one who went to live abroad a couple of months previous. Despite this, I decided to cut down on my drinking and after two years, we made plans to marry. Soon, I felt I was making a mistake, or more to the point, she was making a mistake marrying me. With second thoughts, I tried to restrain from getting married. But when my mother suggested that I could be taken to court for breach of promise, this frightened me. I felt I had lost control of my life. Alcohol and other people were making the decisions for me. The only decision I made was, to get married at Knock Shrine, *and maybe the Blessed Mother would then watch over us.* So I thought.

Soon after getting married, and unable to find full-time employment, I set up my own business carrying out furniture restoration and upholstery, learning the trade as I went along. Starting covering the seats of dining room chairs, pub stools, and any small items of furniture, I could fit onto the back of my Vespa Scooter. I would take them for restoration to the garden shed at the rear of my aunt Kitty's house where my wife and I lived. Eventually I was able to purchase a van to accommodate for much larger items of furniture. One year later, we decided to buy our own house, where I restored and reupholstered the furniture in the spare room. Eventually it became logical that restoring old furniture inside the house wasn't appropriate. I then built a more suitable workshop at the rear of the house.

Two years later, my wife gave birth to our first child, we both were very proud parents. We loved our son dearly. It was at this point, I needed to control my drinking. I was now a father, and had responsibilities. Together, we thoroughly enjoyed family life and enjoyed many outings. We traveled all over Ireland having roadside picnics, going to seaside resorts, and fishing. Nevertheless, I soon started to drink heavy once again, sometimes going to the pub for two weeks at a time without a break, drinking every day. When I could not drink any further, I would stop for a week or two, and do it all over again. Drying out from alcohol was horrible; I had nightmares, and became full of fear. My nervous system had taken a battering from the effects of overindulgence on alcohol.

One sunny afternoon, I had dropped my wife at the entrance to a nearby shopping centre close to where we lived. My two and a half year old son sat in the seat beside me. As I drove around the car park, the afternoon sun dazzled me, and I crashed into a light pole. In an instant, my son was raised from his seat with the sudden impact, heading towards the windscreen. Luckily, my reflex was quick; I had grabbed him in mid air, before he went through the already smashed windscreen. Then there was a puff of smoke and flames immerged from the van's engine, which was directly situated underneath my son's seat. I passed my hysterical son through the window, to a woman who came to our rescue. Luckily, for us the flames subsided, but there was still a strong stench of petrol. Attempting to get out of the van, I was pinned to the seat by the steering wheel. Not alone that, my foot was trapped as well. When I looked down to see where my right foot was trapped, I noticed my ankle was turned to the extreme left by the steering column, in the shape of the letter L. My knee was turned to the extreme right. Next, I remember the atrocious pain, and a flow of weakness come over me. I may have passed out, because next I remembered, there was a crowd of at least one-hundred people surrounding the van, with a loud screaming of sirens in the distance. While the rescue teams were using cutting equipment to rescue me from the van, the pain on my right foot was excruciating. I actually thought that they were cutting off my foot. I yelled at them to stop, however, they reassured me it was the vans panels they were cutting, not my foot. The hospital x-rays confirmed that most of the bones on my ankle were severed. They attached screws to support the bones while they healed. I spent up to three months on crutches. As a result, because I had my own business, there was no choice but to work with the plaster cast on my leg, right up to my hip. It was a very tough time, with no transport for collection and delivering furniture.

More misfortune hit shortly after the plaster cast had been taken off my leg. While helping a friend who had too much to drink, climb the stairs of his house. I lost my balance at the top of the stairs landing, and slipped forward, grapping hold of the banisters railings on the way down. I had dislocated both my shoulders. Too ashamed to go to A&E, I popped in my shoulders with a jolt. As a result, the pain was agonizing for months afterwards.

Another occasion, while making my way home from the pub, I slipped repeatedly on the icy footpath. Each time landing full force directly onto both of my elbows. I suffered in great agony for years afterwards, again too ashamed to go A&E or my doctor. Most people do not have this great extent of misfortune, just because they drank.

Was I cursed, or was I just accident-prone? I questioned repeatedly. Despite this, as long as I was having fun in the pubs, I continued to drink. Eventually alcohol took its toll on my body. I had developed ulcers in my stomach. The moods swings became more frequent. It took its toll on my nervous system, becoming paranoid and fearful of the unknown. I became afraid of everything that moved, even afraid to turn on the television in case it would explode. My concentration was worse than ever. In addition, to make matters worse, my childhood hurts and traumas came back to haunt me. With severe hatred and resentment towards the people who had abused me. The hate and fear I had towards them and my father caused me to wake up, night after night in a deep cold sweat from nightmares, living the past all over again. I became a martyr, and held them responsible for everything bad that had happened to me. If I did not suffer in the hands of those people, my life could have been very different. While I was going through this entire trauma, I felt this drinking had to stop. One evening I met with my friend PJ, and shared with him that I needed to refrain from drinking. He enlightened me about Alcoholics Anonymous (A.A) in which I had never heard of before. After he had explained a little about the meetings, I decided to attend.

At the meetings, I found it problematic to comprehend the lingo they spoke. Most of it seemed like a different language to what I was used of. They spoke about, sincerity, willingness, forgiveness, sobriety, etc. *What was this all about?* I had never heard those words spoken in the pub. It wasn't that they were against alcohol, it was the reality about the effects of alcohol that I failed to fathom. I felt different and failed to fit in and make friends. One way or another, I struggled with life. Stress overpowered me a lot. I could never comprehend why life was such a struggle. From once I got out of bed in the morning, until I go to bed at night. Struggling with almost every task in my life, my marriage, my business, relationships, food, self-respect. Self-loathing was a major one, hating who I had become.

Among the turmoil, I developed an interest to learn how to play the drums. I had acquired drum lesions and got myself a drum kit. What a great way to release stress. Somehow, the draw for alcohol was much greater than the need to quit. After a couple of weeks, I reckoned sobriety was not for me and drew back from the meetings. Days later, I picked up again, thinking I could have fun as I had when I first started drinking. But to my disappointment, the fun had completely gone and it was just doom and gloom, no buzz whatsoever, no matter how much I drank.

By the time I was twenty-seven, I knew if I did not stop drinking I was going to die. By this time, our son was over three-years of age, and I did not want him to see me in the state I was in. Once again, I was hospitalized to be detoxified from alcohol. It was there the doctor became concerned for my health and wellbeing, after he had studied my files. He suggested I attend an alcohol treatment centre. Adding had I no shame, to have such a track record of injuries to my body, most drink related. His advice was, if I did not stop drinking, soon I would be confined to a wheelchair, or dead. In an agreement, he referred me to an alcohol treatment center for four weeks. Like A.A. I attended the four-week program, started to smoke, and learnt a thing or two about the effects of alcohol. Even armed with this knowledge, I felt it may not stop me drinking.

As time went by, my health started to deteriorate, drinking periodically for one or two weeks consistently. Unable to eat or hold down liquids for weeks after stopping drinking, eventually depression had set in, and I was not capable of working. I was unable to take any more. It was after a two-week bender, and sitting at the counter, knowing my life was going nowhere fast. And looking back on my life for the thousandth time, and what a disaster. I was destroying my wife, and my son was beginning to sense there was something wrong, because he would cry a lot when I'd leave the house. While sitting at the counter in a local pub, I wrote a suicide note, tucked it into my pocket, and drank a couple of fast brandies. Saying goodbye to the other customers in the pub, adding, that they would never see me again. Like the barmaid, the customers just nodded, as I left.

On the city street, I accidently bumped into a couple of A.A. members, shook their hands, and bid them farewell. They peered at me suspiciously; as I made my way to the river basin, close by. Knowing I was unable to swim, I climbed up on the steel barrier, and swiftly leaped into the freezing cold water.

Kneeling down in deep mud, at the bed of the basin, I stayed there just waiting to die. Down there was an old bicycle, old tires and what looked like a dead animal, I guess it was somebody's pet dog. Now I was in peace, because in a few seconds it would be all over. No more pain, hate, anger, or violence, those disgusting feeling I had about myself for years had gone. Then a sudden thought came to mind, something somebody at the A.A. meetings had said. He often spoke about the peace and contentment he had in his life since he had stopped drinking. Still immerged underneath the water, I could barely breathe, and had only seconds to live. Figuring if I could stop drinking, and have peace in my life, it could be possible to live a more contented life. I leapt up from the basin bed, and somehow got to the surface. Then I felt somebody grab me by the arm. This person failed to heave me to safety, as the wall surrounding the basin was much too high. I slipped from his grip several times. He had done his upmost to save me. At that time, I had no idea who this person was, but it turned out, years previous, we worked together on the city dockyard. Eventually a rope enters the water. I failed to grab a firm hold on the rope a couple of times. Then I managed to hold a firm grip onto the rope with all of my might. It was members of the local fire brigade, who had thrown me the rope, and had rescued me from drowning. The rest I do not recall, because I was told I was unconscious for over two hours. Afterwards, a friend who was at the scene informed me that a priest from the church close by had anointed me as I lay on the pavement. Others said, I had got dead-mans grip, which literally means, when somebody it dying, sometimes they hold a firm grip onto an object of some kind. In my case it was the the rope, so this is what saved me. I spent one week in hospital, where my body and blood was poisoned by the contaminated waters. When my wife visited me at the hospital with my son, she tossed the local newspaper onto my chest. There was a photograph of me being rescued from the water and another photo with me lying out cold on the pavement. This was rather embarrassing and I felt so ashamed. I was devastated when I learnt that word had spread around the town. Actually, it was revealed to me later that some friends heard rumours that I had died.

On the contrary, I was delighted to be alive, especially for my son. It would have been heartbreaking for him to be brought up without me, because we meant the world to each other. Also my wife, who loved me dearly. It was a very selfish act on my behalf, but when a person is in such a dark place in their live, and see no way out, suicide seems to be a better option. For a while after, I had a certain amount of peace, and I remained sober for over four months, but picked up a drink again. Shaking of the suicidal tendencies was almost impossible. I went on a bender for two-days, and my family was aware of this and pleaded with me to stop drinking. A.A. members called to my house and advised me not to continue drinking that day, and to attend meetings. I wanted to drink so badly that the cravings were unbearable. I refrained from drink on the third day. That evening before entering an AA meeting, an AA friend approached me. He said, if I'd surrender to alcohol, I would never have to suffer or drink again. I knew this to be true. Somehow I felt sobriety was not for me. That was on January 9th 1989. Surprisingly the Good Lord had other plans for me, and up until this present day, with God's help and the help from Alcohol Anonymous; over twenty-seven-years has past, and I have never taken a drink.

Though living sober did not come easy; I was like a fourteen-year old boy trying to live in an adult world. This time, I had to learn how to live life without the crutch of alcohol. Nine-months after I stopped drinking, we had an addition to our family, our baby daughter was born. My love for my two children gave me the strength to carry on. But the negative feelings from being abused never left me, to help with my anxiety; I smoked up to four packets of cigarettes a day. I started to attend counselling with a therapist and attended several twelve-step groups to help me live again, and to come to terms with my childhood traumas. In which it was pointed out that I should stop blaming others for my misfortune and start taking responsibility for my own actions. This was almost impossible to comprehend, since I had myself convinced that everything bad that had happened to me was caused by the guy who abused me, my father, and those who insulted my personal image. At this stage it was time to find out who I was and find my true personality. Somehow it had become apparent that I had gone through life not fully aware of what was going on in the world around me. With lack of interest in politics, religion, economic affairs, I most certainly would not watch the news, or real life documentaries on the television.

My therapist assisted me in understanding my extreme anger. It was a direct result of the traumas I had experienced as a child. Even though I became ashamed of my anger, I thank God for anger, because it was the only way at the time I could express my feelings. People die when they hold life traumas and distress inside oneself. It is very important to share negative experiences with another person or therapist. Although trusting others did not come easy for me, I managed to acquire those I could trust.

Making amends with who I had hurt through my fury and lack of anger control did not come easy either. For one to get inner peace, making restitution is essential for a person's personal recovery. It took a long time before I became interested in politics and economic affairs in our country, including watching the news, and real life documentaries on the discovery channel. Life became more interesting, and satisfactory. I discovered I had an interest to writing, so I jotted down some ideas for books or film. I read a lot about physical health and mental/emotional health. I sought desperately to help other adult children of sexual abuse. Subsequently, another abuse victim had set up meetings in the city for those who were sexual abused. I attended meetings, in which helped me greatly, as a result, I helped him run the meetings to support others victims. What hurt me the most, was when I made amends to my father, he had never apologised for his part in being hostile towards me. When I confronted my abuser, he rejected me, and denied everything, again threatening me if I told anybody about this. Somehow I came to terms with this. It was in the forgiveness, and forgiving myself I felt the most peace. What meant the most to me, was when I was in my early thirties I had hugged my parents for the very first time.

The first four-years of sobriety were rather enjoyable, working on my marriage, taking care of my children, and building up my business. Making new friends, and enjoyed going to listen to bands in the local pubs. It was an amazing experience getting together with a couple of my musician friends and make music. Even if I never played with a band, I thoroughly enjoyed going to live gigs and being invited on stage to drum along to a couple of tunes.

Before long it occurred to me that I was very unhappy in my marriage. It seemed I was living for my wife and children, and as long as they were happy, I became happy. This was wrong, because it made me irate and frustrated. It was time to get honest, and stop lying to myself. I attended a councillor where it was confirmed to me something I already knew, that I did not love my wife. I was living in a loveless marriage. This was no shock to my wife, because in the past I had conveyed this to her many times in an argument. During this time she would ignore me and carried on as usual. Then the disagreements and arguing became more frequent, this was taking its toll on our children. Our marriage started to disintegrate. There was little or no conversation or communication between us. In the fullness of my heart, I knew I could not live with such unhappiness any longer. There was part of me dying inside. I was now thirty-five years old, and life was passing me by without love.

After a painful decision, I decided to leave the family home for a spell, to have time to sort myself out. Now alone in a flat in the city, and not living with my children was tough. Sometimes absence makes the heart grow fonder, missing my wife's company, but I failed to let loneliness drive me back to her. However, our marriage did not end there. I spent a lot of time with my wife and children. We'd go on holidays together, and go on different outings, but the feeling was still the same. To look my wife in the eye and say I love you, never happened. It wasn't in me to love her. Of course I loved her for who she was as a person; but you just cannot force love, it is something that should come naturally. Although we became great friends; sadly living together wasn't to be. I had given up the furniture restoration and upholstery business, and had taken a job driving a tour bus, under-taking private tours around the country. This was thoroughly enjoyable, meeting new people from different countries, who were on holidays. Driving the tour bus felt like it was one long holiday for me too, listening to the guide commentary about local inhabitants in years gone by, culture and past historical events.

Chapter Six

Travel/Adventure & Spiritual Healing

It was the mid-nineties and like drinking my doctor had advised me to quit smoking, because of frequent chest pain I was incurring from smoking eighty cigarettes a day. This was the second hardest challenge ever, after quitting the booze. With the help of the first addition of Alan Car's book, "The Easy Way to Stop Smoking", I eventually quit for good.

I had taken many courses, in acting, film directing, scriptwriting, and had taken part in minor acting scenes on stage and film. Since I already had a flair for writing, this enticed me to write six first drafts of drama/suspense stories, for novels or television. It was then I had the opportunity to meet actor, James Brolin. He was acting and directing an Irish film called "My Brothers War, wherein I was a security guard, and I was featured in the film trailer.

My ambition was, once my children were a little older, I was going to visit a friend in Hollywood Los Angeles. Here I would try my hand at stage plays and the big screen. *Was this a pipe dream?* Who knows? *Would I pursue my career in acting, or had God other plans for me?* I decided to head to England with a friend, for a break. I had the opportunity to visit London for a couple of days. Then travel on to Cambridge, which is a fabulous, vibrant student city. This city is reeking in history with many historical buildings and punting on the river Cam.

While there I had acquired a job driving an open-air top tour bus, on tours of the city. I had some brilliant times meeting different people from all over the world, and especially gaining knowledge of the history of the city. It was enjoyable to have fun and laughter with the tourist. Scientist Stephen Hawking who worked on research at the Centre for Theoretical Cosmology at the University of Cambridge. He claims to have found a hole in the ozone layer. On my route, he would often appear out of one of the many laneways, on his specially adapted wheelchair, and would hold up traffic while crossing the street. While in Cambridge, I attended night classes at Cambridge evening college to brush up on my English and maths. This was thirdly enjoyable, learning prose, words and grammar I wasn't too familiar with.

Sunday afternoons were a favourite occasion for me. At the Boat Race pub, local musicians set up their gear for those who wished to go on stage and jam with them. It was absolutely superb living in Cambridge, except, not seeing my children on a regular basis took its toll. I travelled home a lot to be with them, and eventually after one year I decided to stay home, so I could be close to them.I was delighted when my younger sister Patricia invited me to travel on holidays with her and my parents to visit my brother in Boston. We had a wonderful time, visiting tourist sites, such as the Museum of fine arts and a replica of the pub on Cheers, the popular TV series in the eighties and early nineties. What a wonderful view across the vast city and Boston Harbour from the John Hancock skyscraper.

In the late nineties, I acquired a position as a hackney driver. While driving, I got a suddenly pain across my chest, which ran along my left arm. Not giving it much thought, I continued on working. It was in the oncoming weeks, whenever I would bend over or eat spicy foods; I would experience a severe burning sensation to my chest. After experiencing this pain day in day out for many months, I decided to have it checked out at the local hospital. A doctor diagnosed me as having the symptoms of a Hiatus Hernia. He informed me that he would have to take me into hospital for further diagnosis and carry out a barium study. This consists of a special x-ray that allows visualization of the oesophagus. In the meantime, the doctor prescribed a medicine called Gaviscon to relief the symptoms.

Two and a half years had passed, and I missed several barium study appointments, due to working the night shift. I was cautious with my diet as the doctor suggested. However, almost every day, I encountered a burning sensation to my chest, collapsing a couple of times and losing my breath with the intense pain.

One evening, while visiting my children, and watching a documentary called "Nationwide", on the television about three Irish Spiritual Healers. One of those healers suggested to their viewers who wished to be healed from any illness they might have, to place their hands on the television set. My wife was watching the program and suggested I should leave my hands on the television. At first, I felt embarrassed doing this. Within seconds, a clicking sensation occurred, exactly where I had experienced the burning pain in my chest, most likely caused by a Hiatus Hernia. I told her, that something had clicked inside my chest. Her reply was perhaps your Hernia is been healed. This was doubtful with the lack of faith I had on any sort of spiritual healing.

Sure enough, a couple of weeks had passed; and I finally turned up for the barium examination. After the doctor performed the test on me, he informed me that he could not find any trace of a Hiatus Hernia. I asked him had he detected scar tissue or any signs that I had a Hernia. His reply was, he had not found any scaring. He was amazed when he rechecked my chart and said, I had all the symptoms of a Hiatus Hernia. Somehow, those types of Hernias do not heal by themselves; they would need to be operation on. Straight away, I thought of the three Spiritual Healers, and felt maybe, Jesus Christ had healed me, through those faith healers. That evening I treated myself to hot chicken curry, and felt no pain whatsoever. What a relief, my symptoms had completely vanished.

At this stage I owned my own hackney cab, and after living in different flats from time to time, it was time to own my own house. In early two-thousand, I acquired a mortgage from the bank, and started to build a house on a plot of land my parents had given me years previous. Somehow, it wasn't a good idea going back to live in a village whose people caused me so much grief as a child and teenager. Ignoring this, I carried on regardless and built the house, in the hope those old wounds would not transpire to the surface over again.

A mysterious occurrence had take place while I was working inside the house. I could sense two little blond girls scampering up and down the stairs. They even ran from room to room, giggling and teasing each other. I felt this was strange, and asked myself many times what does this mean. Am I going to have two more children, or could this be the spirits of two deceased girls who may have once lived in the site where I built the house. Even though, I could not see those girls physically, nevertheless their presence was very strong in my spirit.

At first, a small cottage style house was suitable for me to build. But when the builder was marking out the foundation, he laughed at such a tiny house I was building. Therefore, he talked me into building a much larger house, in case one day I would have a family. My view was, *I had no intention of having another family, or could I ever see my ex-wife and children ever living with me in the country. I refused to get myself into a pickle over this.* However, I continued on and finished the house and moved into it. This was the first time I had lived in the countryside for almost twenty-three years. It took time to adapt to the silence, and the fact that after ten-pm most of my neighbours were tucked up in their beds. To add, the local shops were closed at seven-pm. There were times I would discover there was little or no food in the house, and I had to travel into town, thirteen miles away to get groceries.

Pretty soon I got rather fond of living the country lifestyle. There was little or no noisy traffic and I visited my elderly parents almost every day. I enjoyed chatting with them over a cup of tea about different events which occurred over the years, and the radical changes that had taken place in the world, since my father and mother were children. My mother became very informative conveying fond memories about her younger days when she was growing up with her family and friends.

Chapter Seven

My first Pilgrimage to Medjugorje

To my dismay, I had another almost fatal moment. It was on April two-thousand-three, as I was working the night shift as a then taxi driver. I had just picked up a fare of two male students at the taxi rank in the city and proceeded to take them to their destination. At this stage, I had lost interested in my choice of employment and like thousands of times previous to this, I pondered on how I was going to get away from taxi driving and pursue my career as an actor/writer.

Then suddenly another motorist came across my path, leaving me with no choice but to crash into their car. I was thrown forward, and from side to side. Screaming for their lives, were my two passengers. Then I felt an enormous blow to the left side of my head. My head had collided with one of the passenger's head who was sitting beside me. My car bounced furiously two or three times, finally coming to a halt imbedded into the drivers' door of the car that drove across my path.

For a moment or two, I was dazed, and as I opened my eyes I noticed the front of my car had caught fire. The passengers evacuated the car as quick as they could. My left knee had locked in a stiff position and the pain was excruciating, as it did for years after the accident in the public house. I then had difficulty unfastening my safety belt, since it became jammed. Watching the front of the car being engulfed in flames, panic started to set in, but to my relief I managed to unleash the seatbelt buckle and get out of the inflamed car as quickly as possible. I wept as I watched the car being almost taken over by flames. Then a thought came to mind, that I go back inside the car, to retrieve my phone and some mortgage money, I had placed underneath the seat. Even though, I wasn't the religious type, I remembered a relic of Saint Padre Pio, which was given to me by my mother. She had been adamant I'd carry this relic in my car at all times. She said, she felt I needed something consecrated to protect me, since I spent a considerable amount of time on the road. I made a dash to the car, and managing to retrieve the relic from the panel of the driver's door panel, my phone and mortgage money which was beneath the driver's seat.

As I watched my car go up in flames, I shuddered at the horrific memory, as to when I arrived at the scene of an accident, months previous. A young Traveller couple's car had crashed into a stone wall, and their car had caught fire. The driver managed to get his wife out of the car, but could not unfasten his own safety belt. People at the scene tried to save him, but it was too late. They were overpowered by smoke and flames, and the young man died as a result. Later I had learnt that the young couple were on their way home from a twenty-first birthday party, a party I had dropped several people too, earlier that night. I shivered in horror to think this could have happened to me. I was grateful to be alive. By the time the fire brigade arrived, my car was engulfed in flames. Next morning, when I woke up I was in so much pain, it felt I had been driven over by a bus. Where those aches and pains came from, I had no idea at first. I had been awake for at least a half-an-hour before I remembered the accident the night before. Even though the accident could have been fatal, I wept because my business had gone up in smoke. Then I received a phone call from my friend Christopher, asking me was I still alive. I was shocked when he told me I phoned him at three in the morning. Apparently he had gotten out of bed and had taken me to the hospital, where he said a doctor examined me and carried out some tests and an x-ray to my left wrist. My only memory of this was a flash moment standing in the waiting room in the A&E department. What shocked me the most, was when Christopher conveyed to me, he had driven me home, and slept in my house for a couple of hours, before he proceeded on his way to work.

In the upcoming weeks, I got another taxi car up and running. But what frightened me the most was that I had very little memory of the days and weeks following the accident. I became moody, agitated and struggled to get back to fulltime work. I could only manage to work a couple of hours per week. My attention span became weak as time went by. Leaving my house became an unpleasant task. Interacting with family and friends became a laborious undertaking. The horrific thoughts came to the fore, of the moment my father had said I would never have a day's luck ever again, because of the arguments we were having. Eventually after three months, I visited a Psychiatrist where he diagnosed me as suffering from post-traumatic stress. Now that I knew what was wrong with me, I could do something about it.

As I looked back at my life of accidents and misfortune, I could not help wondering, had my father cursed me. *Could this be the cause of my misfortune?* Not sure was there such thing as a curse, however, the isolation and emptiness became unbearable. Being depressed and lying on the couch, flicking channels on the telly was as much as I could accomplish.

A lot of my opinions about people and places became distraught and negative, which rubbed off on my family and friends. Fury had showed its ugly head once again and became a major issue. It seems letting off steam became a foremost survival kit. Once again, childhood and teenage hurts began to taunt my mind. Even though I had dealt with those issues that haunted me in the past, things like the abuse, bulling, name calling and many insults which had been made about my physical appearance. In any case, I failed to shake off the sentiment. Spending time with my children became problematic since I rarely left the house. To add to my unhappiness, I developed asthma, and had a major operation on my sinuses, whereby I spent three days in hospital. Following this, I had lost my sense of smell. Unaware of this at the time, but it was made known to me that my parents worried considerably, as to how my personality had changed dramatically. They could see I was not my cheerful self. Thinking this change to my personality may have something to do by the fact that I was separated from my wife and children. Also they knew I had filed for a divorce. At the time, divorce was unheard of in our family. My parents, my sister Patricia, and friends had intervened, and advised me to make an effort, and reconcile with my wife. I had done this many times over a nine-year period, but to no avail, knowing that the definition of insanity was, trying the same thing over and over again, expecting different results.

My wife had suggested we both should travel to Medjugorje, and maybe I might view our marriage differently afterwards. Despite the fact that I felt my Hiatus Hernia had been healed by God, I had no interest in going anywhere near a religious or holy place. We had got married at Knock Shrine, and a fat lot of good that was to our marriage.

It was mid-August, I wanted out. Suicide had come to the fore once again. After securing a rope to the rafters, and had made a noose to tie around my neck. Just as I was about to jump from the attic door, a car drove into the driveway. Then I could hear somebody in the kitchen calling out "hello". Dazed and muddled, I went down stairs to the kitchen. It was my youngest sister Patricia. Over a cup of tea, she suggested I should travel with her to a Life in the Spirit Seminar at the house of prayer at a country village called Finny Clonbur, in North West Galway. This house of prayer is run by Breda Laffey who was cured from cancer by a miracle, years earlier. When I asked her why should I go there, she said that she worried about me, because of my negative attitude, and she felt I needed prayers. She may have a point, after all I was about to end my life, which I then postponed. She had persuaded me to visit the house of prayer with her the following evening. I had no idea what this was all about?

We arrived there just as mass was about to be celebrated. Through the entire mass, my heart was pounding since I couldn't wait for it to end. Afterwards, Breda, who spoke with a firm voice, and appeared to be a robust type of woman, spoke about those who dealt in Reiki, angel cards, yoga and the occult and living a new age life. "You are dealing with the devil himself", she insisted. Wow, this seemed powerful and deep, but did I believe her? After all I had never dealt in such activities. Then she spoke about, anger, rage and demonic curses. Following this, she had my attention. As she spoke about curses she stared right into my eyes, while I stood in the aisle, in the centre of the room.

She continued to converse about the effects of curses, and drew closer to me, making eye contact. I felt she knew I may have been cursed. How could she know this? Then I thought, *had I confided this to my sister or family, and they passed this information on to her*? Most likely that was the case. Or it could have only been a coincidence, or did she see something demonic in me? For days afterwards, I deliberated on what Breda had said, was all my misfortune caused by a curse? I thought about all the misfortune I had suffered in my life, not to mention the three cars, two van's, and a bus that had caught fire as I was driving them. *Was I jinx or what?*

Over the coming weeks, Patricia would call to my house, and talk about different houses of prayer. I tried to persuade her that I do not need to go to any other house of prayer, mass or confession. I told her to go away and leave me alone. I thought she would never give up. Then she asked me to go on a pilgrimage with a group of people from the city. She said that our parents were worried about me, since I was not visiting them as much as I used to, and infrequently left my house. I was reluctant to travel with her, since my religious beliefs were, *as long as you do good for others, and try not to harm anybody, most likely a person would be on the right side of God, and get into heaven.*

Repeatedly, she insisted I'd travel with her on this pilgrimage, to a place where the Blessed Virgin was appearing near Croatia. She felt Our Lady had chosen us to travel there. It was a place called Medjugorje. Yeah sure, I had little or no interest in this whatsoever. Nor did I care to believe that Our Lady was appearing there, neither did I feel the need to learn anything about it. It so happened after a week or two, I gave in to her persistence, and agreed to meet with her at the Galway Cathedral. We joined up with the remainder of the group who were travelling to Medjugorje. As we boarded the coach, I truly had second thoughts with reference to this trip. Apprehensively I gazed around at the group of people; most of them were a lot older than I. The majority of them were married couples, and here I was separated, unattached, had filed for a divorce and an annulment, and was feeling absolutely awful. All of which were not in favour by the Catholic Church. *What would those people think of me?* I dreaded the thought. I was emotionally embarrassed, ashamed of who I was, and was conscious as to who might see me board a coach with what I felt was a group of Holy Joes, heading off on pilgrimage.

Then to put a spanner in the works, Bernard and his wife who were my former neighbours turned up along with his brother Alfie, plus another two guys, John and Murt. I knew them for many years. I had no idea how I was going to explain to them, why I was going on this trip, since I felt they might have already known I was not entirely religious. Shame and disloyalty to my faith, had overpowered my thoughts.

After all, I had not gone to mass or confession in almost twenty-years. I felt an imposter amongst those folks, and was pretty sure most of them were regular mass goers. Once the coach began its journey to Shannon Airport, the rosary beads were taken out, and the bus microphone was handed to Father Martin Keane from the parish of Clarinbridge Co Galway. In which I was to learn, he was our spiritual leader. He sat at the front seat of the coach, and started to recite the rosary. At this point, I almost had thrown a tizzy. I took one look at my sister and asked, "where in the name of God are you taking me? This is crazy; those people are saying the rosary on a bus."

And, of course her reply was, "it is your choice; you do not have to join in on the prayers, if you don't wish too." Then she ignored me and joined in on the prayers. I felt I wanted to get off this crazy bus, and get away from those people, but was too embarrassed to even make a move or create a scene. Subsequently, memories of a religious experience I'd had years previous, clouded my mind, when a person claimed to be holy. He prayed over me, it was an experience I felt went wrong, and frightened me a great deal. I was in a zombie state for a couple of days. It felt as if I was hypnotised. Even though, it was rather a calming experience, I was attending mass every day and constantly praying. It felt as if I was a Jehovah Witness. Somehow this was not for me.

As the others on the coach continued to pray, somehow I managed to focus my attention on the trip ahead. Wondering what this foreign country would be like. Deciding that this trip was going to be a holiday, and I marvelled about the native people and their traditions. Still not entirely sure at to what country we were visiting. Nonetheless, the coach continued with me still on it. We arrived at the Airport; we began to check in our luggage. As I gaped around at the many bewildered faces, and some were rather jolly, as they told me, they had visited Medjugorje many times before. Most of them believed the Blessed Virgin was appearing there. Though, it was fascinating to hear this, *but is it true*. I speculated, *and did I believe it?*

It was at this point, I was introduced to the three group leaders, Lesley, Michael and Tony, and of course, Father Martin Keane. Now that I was introduced to those people, who seemed to be well acquainted with my sister, I felt there was no going back. I began to loosen up and engaged in conversation with John, Alfie and his brother Bernard, asked questions about this place we were travelling to. Except they were reluctant to say anything about it, just that the scenery was beautiful, and that the climate is very hot. Bernard said he was there a couple of times before. The rest shrugged their shoulders at any other questions I reluctantly asked, and they turned to chat amongst themselves. *What a peculiar group of old fogies,* I thought, *and why are they so secretive about this place called Medjugorje.*

Nonetheless, we boarded the plane and we were on our way to a city I had never heard of before; it was called Split in Croatia. After all, here was a forty-three year old man travelling half way across Europe, and had no idea what was ahead of him. On the airplane, I sat next to Patricia, she explained to me how in 1981, the Blessed Mother appeared to six children at the foot of a mountain. And still does on a daily basis to this present day. She had already told me this, *but what a load of baloney,* I thought. Looking over my shoulder towards John, Alfie and Bernard, questioning their sanity, *had those guys belief in this twaddle as well*? For years previous to this, I had not spent a great deal of time with my sister. I began to wonder, *that she might be a bit batty. So if she was batty, so was everybody else on the plane.* A cold shiver ran down my spine. I shuddered with the thought, *that I could have boarded a plane with a group of escapees from a loony bin, somewhere in the west of Ireland.*

Eventually, three hours later, the plane touched down at Split airport. It was dark and very warm when we entered a coach to take us to our destination. We travelled for over two hours or so, with very little scenic views to see through the darkness. Finally the bus pulled over. Tony our group leader informed us that we had arrived at some border or other. I noticed the military, and some armed police officers approach the bus. We were asked to vacate the bus and hand over our passports. We were all in shock by this procedure. Tony reassured us that the military officers had not done this in a while. *What did he mean by "a while?"* That was when I glanced over my shoulder to notice a sign stating "You Are Now Entering Bosnia & Herzegovina". I then paled of the images that raced through my mind of the war in Bosnia, after the breakup of Yugoslavia in the early nineties. I nodded to Patricia, to glance over her shoulder to read the large sign behind her. "O Vincent," she said, "Bosnia? Is this where we are?"

"Is that all you have to say. Do you realise this is a war stricken country?" I extremely snapped, thinking, *we might never make it back to Ireland alive.* In any case, all went well. We were given back our passports, and were on our way.

We arrived late that night at our guesthouse in Medjugorje. For some unknown reason, I felt a since of inner peace and tranquillity. Then we were booked in to our rooms by Sandra, the proprietor of the guesthouse. The next morning, I rose at nine-thirty to greet the unknown day ahead. The rest of the group had already left at daybreak to climb one of the mountains, in which I had no intention of doing. To cut to the chase, climbing mountains at six-thirty in the morning was not my idea of fun, because I had breathing difficulties, and a wonky knee. Still feeling bushed after the journey the day before; I entered the cafeteria and experienced an encounter with a glorious apparition who instantly stole my heart. The waitress behind the counter greeted me with a glorious and glowing smile. My heart skipped a beat with great joy. In that instant I felt that this young gorgeous woman would be the one I would want to marry, and spend the rest of my life with. She served me a late breakfast, and her smile, impaled in my heart repeatedly. Was this love at first sight? I was soon deflated, figuring I could be old enough to be her father. Brushing off the notion, and gathering my thoughts as she approached me and then served me a coffee. With a glowing smile, she asked me was I from Ireland, and why hadn't I climbed the mountain with the rest of the group. She laughed at my retort about the mad notion, climbing mountains at six-thirty in the morning. I marvelled behind her smile, had she many skeletons in the closet, or was she as innocent as she appeared.

Through the dining room window, she pointed out Mount Crivis, known as Cross Mountain, where the group had climbed. I had no idea who she was or how old she was. Even though we were two worlds apart, and a picture paints a thousand words, something told me I had not seen the last of her. After breakfast, and with her glowing beam and her soft-spoken European accent, still infixed in my thoughts. I faced out into the day ahead, and the intense heat of thirty-two degrees. Seeing the countless grapevines and countless olive trees scattered across the valley, surrounded by the picturesque mountain terrain, including the hills and mountains. A sense of joyfulness had once again pierced my heart with great inner peace.

As I strolled along the narrow path from the guest-house, I noticed my memory became almost transparent, recalling all conversations of the trip. It seemed all my worries were over. Of course it became obvious to me that one might feel in high spirits and more tranquil, once they were on holidays and away from their every-day struggles in life. Nonetheless, somehow this seemed different. I was free for the first time in my life. I could never imagine in a million years, being this free could feel so liberating. No worries about work, finances, chil-dren, past life, or responsibilities.

Tears of joy streamed down my face, as I jollied along the pathway. I noticed an elderly lady, native I guessed, rolling large dried leaves into a roll. Her tanned and craggy skin complexion almost equalled the same texture as the dried leaves she was rolling. As I watched her for a moment, it became apparent she was rolling tobacco leaves into a handmade cigar. It was revealed to me afterwards, along with wine making, growing to-bacco was a source of a vital income in this region.

Moving on, and reading a pamphlet about the vil-lage, which was given to me by the kind waitress, in which I had neglected to introduce myself, or even ask her name. As a rule, it is most impolite to ask a lady her age, of which I was eager to find out. I began to specu-late what I was doing here in these foreign lands. The most pondering thoughts on my mind at the time, was, *what had Medjugorje in store for me? Why had I come here?* I had heard on the coach, from our group leader Lesley, and Patricia, that Our Lady, Queen of Peace, gives us a calling to visit this Holy Land. *Had she chosen me?* I wondered, *and why?* Or was I just a victim of my own uncertainty, since I was not able to convince my younger sister, that I had no business visiting Medjugorje. After all, I had given in to her countless text messages, phone calls and calling to my residence to convince me that I ought to travel with her on this pilgrimage. As she probably felt at the time, it would be beneficial to me. Most likely she was thinking my divorce proceedings were taking its toll, and brought on my depression.

Chapter Eight

Visiting Saint James Church

Strolling along the narrow pathway, I could see among the giant palms trees, two large steeples nuzzled between the foothills. Drawn closer, I could now see the stone construction of Saint James Church. At first, I was reluctant to enter the grounds of the church, but exhaustion from the sweltering heat had forced me to find a suitable place to rest. Therefore, I figured the church might be an appropriate place to escape the sweltering heat. Meandering outside the church for a moment, in case Bernard, or the others may be lurking about and see me enter the church. However, the heat had overpowered me, and I had no choice but to enter.

As I gradually entered, a man and a woman speaking in German accents were about ten-feet to my right. As I was going to take a rear seat, I experienced a thump to the centre of my back, right between my shoulder blades. I could feel the force of an impression of a human hand between my shoulders. This startled me greatly. My immediate reaction was to turn around and have it out with the German guy entering behind me. Because initially I thought he may have thumped me for some strange reason. I was conscious of the other people present at the other end of the church, who may have been watching me get the thump from this guy. As I turned around, the German guy, and the young female were at least twenty-feet to my right. Unless he had a lengthy arm, or he was a fast sprinter, there was no way on earth; he or the female could have touched me. I thought this blow to my back was peculiar. Just as I was going to take a seat; I experience a second thump between my shoulders blades, this time the thump was somehow a slight bit softer than the first. Bewildered, an pressing thought came to my mind that I should take a seat at the top of the church. I proceeded along the centre aisle, and sat four seats from the top, on the right hand side.

And almost immediately, I noticed, slowly appearing on the tabernacle door, was an image of Saint Padre Pio. In which he was facing towards the statue of the Blessed Virgin Mary. At first I thought it was a portrait image with some special effects so that it could appear in front of the tabernacle. But it seemed to be afloat in mid air, and not attached to anything.

Removing my glasses, thinking the lenses might be playing tricks with my eyesight, or maybe it may be mist on the lenses, after I entered the cool air. With my glasses off, I could still see the image. I wiped my eyes, and the lenses, put my glasses back on, and to my surprise the image of Padre Pio was still present. I looked around the church to see had anybody else witnessed this. People were sitting contentedly saying their prayers, some reading the Bible, while others read from prayer booklets. I begin to think that this could be some kind of gimmick to entice people to believe Saint Padre Pio was appearing in Medjugorje, along with the Blessed Mother. I thought this was ridiculous, it was going a little too far, displaying a 3D like image of Padre Pio on the tabernacle by some sort of camera projector. Looking around for a projector, I could not find one. I stayed seated and staring intently at Padre Pio's image. *Why had Padre Pio appeared to me?* I pondered. *Or why couldn't this image have been the Blessed Virgin?*

As I looked intently at the image, a pressing urge was pounding in my heart. It was an urge that was not quite my own, it seemed almost like a soft spoken voice. It was to visit Our Lady's statue, which was to my right, the statue Saint Padre Pio was facing. After staring at the image for one hour, I then left my seat, and stood in front of the statue of Our Lady with countless other people who were praying. It was wonderfully decorated with countless vases of freshly white Lilies and other decorative flowers. For a moment, I glanced across at the tabernacle, but the image of Padre Pio was no longer visible. As I turned to face Our Lady, I noticed she had the most beautiful glowing smile, I had ever seen.

Shocked to see this, at first I thought it was a mask somebody had quickly placed there. This would be impossible, because I had only turned my head for an instant. I felt so serene and joyful somehow my heart was full with joy and love. The emptiness I felt in my heart for many years had vanished. Somehow, I was inhibited to say anything to the others around me. I felt compelled to go down on my knees. Praying for about a half a hour, the Our Father, ten Hail Mary's, and glory Be to the Father, over and over again. Going out into the church grounds, I was amazed with what I had witnessed. I brooded over, *should I mention this to the others in the group, or should I keep it to myself?* Deciding it may be best to keep it to myself for now. Not sure was I hallucinating, or was it just a figment of my imagination, or an optical illusion? Or could it have been a miracle? After all, I did carry a relic of Saint Padre Pio in my car, which may have saved my life from countless car accidents I could have been involved in as at late night taxi driver. The most amazing thing about this experience was, suicide had never crossed my mind ever again.

I knew very little about Father Padre Pio, only he had received the stigmata of Jesus Christ, for most of his life. Later, after reading about his life, he was a priest at San Giovanni Rotondo Southern Italy, until his death in 1968. Curious, and eager to learn more, I was intrigued to learn, that Father Pio, whose devotion to our Blessed Mother is one of his most outstanding characteristics. Also he was cured from pleurisy by Our Lady of Fatima. His last words before he died were, Maria, Gesu, Maria, which means Jesus Mary. Then he passed away. *Is there a message in this for me?* I began to believe that there was a spiritual supernatural phenomenon at work here. This is a special prayer from Father Padre Pio. "Renew your faith in the promises of eternal life which our most sweet Jesus makes to those who fight energetically and courageously. You should be encouraged and comforted by the knowledge that we are not alone in our sufferings, for all the followers of Nazarene scattered throughout the world suffer in the same manner and are all exposed like ourselves to the trials and tribulations of life. Prayer is the best weapon we have; it is the key to God's heart.

You must speak to Jesus not only with your lips, but with your heart. In fact on certain occasions you should only speak to Him with your heart."

I then purchased a writing pad and a booklet in the church bookshop nearby. Written on the booklet were Our Lady's apparitions and messages. I read about how many people began to gather to pray at the foot of Mount Podbrdo immediately after the first apparition of the Madonna. First the local parishioners and then people from other villages nearby, who started to gather, and go on their knees to pray. Soon, and thanks to Our Blessed Mother Mary, Medjugorje, which was a sleepy village parish, became a place of gathering for a multitude of pilgrims from around the world. Attracting fifty-million pilgrims, now Medjugorje is one of the largest prayer centres in the entire world, comparable to Lourdes and Fatima. Countless witness's testimonies reveal, they have found God and peace in their hearts from the blessings they have received by visiting Medjugorje.

It was then I met up with the remainder of the group, who had climbed Mount Crivis, in the early hours. They were by the side of the church, surrounding a female guide who spoke intensely about how God sent Our Blessed Mother to earth. Her mission is to convert and have all mankind believe they must not suffer, because Her Son suffered and died on the cross for each and every one of us. I listened for a short moment, before sneaking away for a coffee into a nearby restaurant. While there, I jotted down a couple of notes on my experience in the church. Soon two female members from an American group sat next to me. We started to chat. They asked me how my day was going and what my views on Medjugorje were. I desperately wanted to share my experience with them, but refrained.

One of them spoke about how she was a witness to the Blessed Mother. I had no idea what this meant. When I asked, her replied was, the Blessed Mother had appeared to her on Apparition Hill, a couple of years earlier. Ever since, her life has changed for the better. Somehow I wanted to believe her, but is this realistic. I was reluctant to converse my experience in the church in case they made a scene. So if I refrained from believing her, who was going to believe me?

Noticing the time on the church clocks, I headed for the guesthouse to have a short nap before evening supper at five. I hadn't thought a great deal about the friendly waitress during the day; however, when I entered the cafeteria I was greeted once again by her glowing smile. She asked me would I like to join her for a coffee. It was then I introduced myself, stretching out my arm. We shook hands and she introduced herself as Violeta. Nervously, I sat at one of the tables. So here I was shaking in my pants, not having a clue how I was going to interact with this young lady. What was I going to say? Then as she placed two coffees on the table, she didn't beat around the bush, the questions started to flow. What did I work at? Was I married with children, and how old was I? I was to learn she was no teenager, she had two daughters, Sandra aged nine, and Anita aged six. Then out of the blue, her shocking story floored me, when she revealed she had been widowed at the tender age of twenty-six. She was from north Bosnia, and her husband was ran over by a car, and died at the scene. It was on the second of June, the same date but different years, I was knocked down by a car, and my father-in-law had died on that date also. Her birthday was on the 28th of August and mine was on the 31st. What a coincidence. I was taken aback by this. It seemed her life was no bed of roses; regardless she laughed and smiled a great deal. We chatted for a while, and I began to feel very comfortable in her company. I could sense great chemistry between us; it was like we were two birds of a feather. It seemed we had a lot in common. The other pilgrims in our group began to enter. One of them had a camera, thus Violeta and I willingly posed for a snapshot. Soon after, I made my way to evening mass and services. I also made my first confession in almost twenty-years. It was a strange and fearful moment. I confessed a couple of minor sins. The priest recommended I return to my faith, and go to confession on a regular basis. He gave me penance and absolution. It was a great feeling to break the fear I had for years of going to confession.

Next morning, I attended mass with the group. I sat on the same seat as the day before when I witnessed Padre Pio on the tabernacle. The church was packed to capacity, with ornamental bouquet of flowers at the front of the altar, and surrounded the statue of our Lady. Then the church choir started to sing a beautiful hymn called "Thank You Jesus". And to my amazement, at least over twenty priests from different countries and parishes from around the world, walked out on to the altar. My only memory from the homily that morning was, the priest who celebrated mass was Father John Chisholm, who was Medjugorje's resident English speaking priest. He spoke about, handing our will and our lives over to God. I had heard this mentioned before, many times at twelve step groups, but never could apply it to my personal life. I was overjoyed to receive the Body and Blood of Jesus Christ through the Holy Eucharist for the first time in years. It was at this moment the seed was sown, somehow I was overwhelmed with guilt, that I regretted not attending holy mass for so many years. I decided to try and put the shame of not being religious or holy behind me. I set out to get involved with the group, and attended every other services and events for the remainder of the coming week.

After mass, the entire group visited the community of Cenacolo, which is a centre for those who have fallen into drugs and addiction. It was founded by Sister Elvira Petrozzi in 1983, to reach out to young people who had taken a wrong path in life. There are other similar houses of Cenacolo throughout Italy, France, Croatia, Bosnia-Herzegovina, Ireland, Brazil, Austria, Dominican Republic, USA (Florida) and Mexico. That afternoon, I made my way to the Adoration Chapel. The chapel is located at the rear of the confessionals, heading towards the passageway. It was built in 1981. It is a place for silent adoration of the most Sacred Heart of Jesus in the Most Blessed Sacrament, and is present on the Altar to all pilgrims and parishioners. In the afternoon, the Chapel is usually open for silent personal prayer, following the morning masses celebrated in many different languages from pilgrims groups worldwide.

Kneeling in front of the Blessed Sacrament, I felt all the stresses, anxieties and pressures of life overpower me like it had done over and over again; as far back as I could remember. Worries about finances, my future, my children, my marriage, and a million other qualms which bombarded my thoughts on a daily bases. For what seemed like hours and hours, tears streamed down my face with the intense pressures of my life. In which somehow after suffering those pressures once again, I felt compelled to hand my will and my life over to the care of God. A sense of inner peace came over me once again as I let go of the frustrating task to control my life. It was at this point I felt all my struggles in life could be made much easier. Now I felt it is up to the Good Lord to lead me from here on in, and that I resign from running my own life. A sense of freedom had come over me. As the old saying goes, "one will only listen, when one is ready." At this stage of my life, I was more than willing to change and trust in the goodness in God.

That evening, I was heading to the village with two others from our group, when a local taxi pulled over. There were four other group members inside the taxi. My neighbour Murt lowered the window and said they were going on a trip, and suggested I'd join them. Without thinking, I got into the already crowded taxi. Little did I know where we were going? It was to climb Cross

Mountain. Worried, I conveyed to Murt I cannot climb this mountain. I am an asthmatic, have a severe sinus infection, in which my breathing is limited, and my left knee kept locking, following an old injury. Ultimately Murt and the other guys talked me into climbing the mountain.

Without my asthma inhaler, we started to climb, and for our intentions, prayed the rosary at each of the Station of the Cross. I actually thought I would not make it to the top of the mountain, as I was gasping to breathe, but somehow I made it. It was amazing to touch the large cross at the summit. The fabulous view across Medjugorje and beyond was breath taking. It was then I felt God's presence, without-a-doubt it was He who helped me make it to the large cross at the summit. We recited the Holy Rosary, before we made our decent.

Early next morning, our entire group, along with thousands of other pilgrims, crossed the grapevines towards Vicka's parent's house, to hear her give her testimony. The house is close to Apparition Hill and the Blue Cross. There were thousands of people present. She spoke about the very first time she had witnessed the Madonna up on the hill. And before Our Lady's visits, she only prayed out of habit. And since the Blessed Mother has chosen her as her witness, she has turned completely to prayer, and committed her life to God. She says she feels sorry for those people who do not believe in God, because Our Lady wants no one to be lost.

Jotting this down, this made me ashamed to be catholic, *would I take a leaf from her book, or would I carry on my old ways when I got back home,* I deliberated on this. To be honest at this stage, like the American woman in the restaurant, I wasn't entirely convinced the Blessed Mother was appearing to Vicka. But I was willing to give her the benefit of the doubt.

During evening rosary, I was mystified as to why so many people were staring directly at the sun, and saying "woooow" and blessing themselves. *Couldn't this have caused damage to their eyesight?* Because I would undoubtedly get headaches whenever I was driving with the sun glaring through the windscreen. That evening, at dusk our group visited Apparition Hill. I noticed the rocks were worn down, most likely from all the people who had walked on them. Even though I wasn't favourable of large groups, I began to feel more comfortable with the group and started to interact with most of them. I began to lighten up and I started to feel at one with them. Indeed it was more beneficial to me, by having a better desire to be by myself, rather than try to fit in.

We prayed the Holy Rosary and sang some beautiful hymns. Later we made our way back down the hill to the Blue Cross, which is situated at the foot of Mount Podbdrdo. Again we prayed the Holy Rosary and sang hymns. I was amazed with my sister's beautiful singing voice. She conveyed to me that this was the very first time she has ever sung in her entire life. She never realised she had a singing voice. And the most amazing miracle of all is, up until this present day of two-thousand-sixteen, she now sings and plays the guitar at church and at prayer group meetings. Also a couple of members of the group, who had visited Medjugorje many times previous to this, gave their testimonies. One man spoke about how he was addicted to gambling, alcohol and drugs. And since he visited to Medjugorje the first time, he found the strength through Jesus, to overcome his addictions.

Others shared how they had turned their backs on the church and the Lord for many years, and now they have received conversion. They attend mass and confession on regular basis. Those stories intrigued me, and gave me something to reflect on, that one day maybe I could change my ways and serve the Lord. Tony, one of our group leaders shared how he got a beautiful scent of roses, at a prayer meeting at a friend's house. Adding, that this was a sign that the Blessed Mother Mary was present. I wasn't too sure whether to believe this or not. Although I had my own experiences in the church a couple of days previous. I felt the need to analyse this further. At this stage, it was dark; and visibility was only two to three feet in front of us. Even though most of us had flash lights, the steep slippery rocks were a challenge for most of the elders in the group. "Never mind," a gentle voice uttered among the crowd. "Our Lady will soon light up the darkened path, so we can all make our way to the bottom of the hill safely."

I recognised this voice as my neighbour, Bernard. He added that the Blessed Mother Mary would never leave us stranded in the darkness. And Lord-be-hold, to our amazement the clouds opened, exactly where the almost full moon was positioned in the darkened sky.

It was almost as bright as day. All I could hear from across the entire group was a loud "woooow" and other voices from a distance, said, "that this was a miracle". "Praise the Lord", a soft voice had expressed in the crowd. This was my sister Patricia.

On our descent, I caught up with Bernard, and asked him, how did he know that the Blessed Mother would light up the skies. "Just trust in Her," was his response, with a casual smile. During breakfast next morning, I chatted with our Spiritual Leader, Father Keane. It was at this time I conveyed to him that I cannot comprehend all this religious conviction. That I wasn't sure Our Lady was appearing to the visionaries. And how some people insist, if one is not a good catholic, they may not get into heaven. "Of course being a good Catholic may increase our chances in getting into heaven," he said, "on the other hand, being a good Christian is what the Lord expects from us," he added. He also reassured me, once I learned more about Our Lady's visitations; I would most likely believe She is appearing to the visionaries. Even if, his guidance was short and to the point, I gave it a great deal of thought.

Later, we went on a bus trip to Siroki Brijeg, to hear Father Jozo speak. All I jotted down from his talk was how some people, who had made money and property their God, were most likely very unhappy and discontented people. Those of us who choose God, and follow the scriptures, receive His fruits and blessings. Thus, they live most happy and contented lives. Then he began to pray, and laying hands on people. Some would fall to the floor. I learnt this was resting in the Holy Spirit. I was determined not to fall to the floor when he laid his hands on me. As Father Jozo lay his hands over me and prayed, with all my might I resisted. Then I felt a strange intense energy passing through my body. A warm glowing sensation that felt like pins-needles rushed through my body, from head to toe. Beginning to feel weak, my knees began to buckle. Just as I was about to collapse in weakness, to the floor, he moved on to the next person. I slammed to the floor, and rested in the Holy Spirit. Not sure how long I lay there, but when I got to my feet, I felt different inside, cleansed almost; it was if something miraculous had entered my body. At first, I thought it could have been high blood pressure, or having a reaction to the heat, even though it was rather chilly inside the church.

In the course of the evening, this warm glow rushed through my entire body. I decided to convey this to a couple of priests, and one of our group leaders called Lesley. They suggested it could have been a miracle, or I may have received the gift of healing through Jesus Christ. *The gift of healing,* I feared. I really did not want anything like this. Back home people would think I maybe weird it they found out. Yet again, I was letting shame overshadow any belief or trust, I had in God. That night, entering the cafeteria of our guest house, the entire group were formed. Lesley asked me to take a seat and reveal to the group about my experience. There was no way I was revealing this in public, and said I was tired, and made a quick dash for the stairs leading to my bedroom. Lying in bed, the ceiling overhead started to change colour. A greyish type figure started to appear. Scared; I closed my eyes and prayed for this to stop. *Am I going crazy, or is this a hallucination.* Upon opening my eyes, the figure was still there. It was clear it was a figure of a woman wearing a shawl or a veil. "Is this you Our Lady?" I cried. "Please don't appear to me, as I cannot handle this." Within a flash the figure had disappeared. *Oh my God, what is happening to me? Am I going crazy? Or has somebody spiked my tea? Or is this how Our Lady is appearing to the visionaries?*

Next morning, it was a privilege to convey to our spiritual leader, Father Keane, my experiences in the church with Saint Padre Pio, and with Father Jozo. Ready for a long sermon to resolve my confusion, his answer was brief and direct. He advised me not to analyse it too much, that the Good Lord will show me the way. He said that Our Lady chooses who comes to Medjugorje, and maybe the Lord has chosen me to be a healer of Christ. And that Saint Padre Pio could have chosen me to be one of his children. *I'm not sure about that,* I thought. *Maybe time will tell.* When I conveyed to him that I had filed for a divorce and annulment, and how God would never chose me to be a healer. His reply was, "that God does not judge. That one day He will reveal to me why he had chosen me to be a child of Saint Padre Pio". *Powerful stuff,* I thought, but was I ready for this assignment? Then we attended morning mass at Mothers Village, which is an orphanage that was set up by the late Father Slavko Barbaric, during the conflict.

That evening I received confession for the second time in almost twenty-years. This time I decided to hold nothing back about my sins in the past. Afterwards I felt a great burden was raised from my mind. After supper that evening, I lay in by bed, suddenly the door slammed open. It was a very excited Patricia. She beckoned me to hurry to the balcony, to watch the sun. I joined her out in the balcony, and Lord-be-hold, the sun was doing a dance in the sky, close to Cross Mountain.

"Isn't this wonderful", Patricia cried, with her hands joined and tears streaming down her face. "Praise the Lord. This was one of Our Lady's signs, that she is present here in Medjugorje." she added.

Most likely she was right, but I was sure dumfounded with what I had just witnessed. The most amazing think was, when she said the time was twenty-minutes to seven. This is the exact time the Madonna appear to Vicka. That evening the entire group went along to a concert in the yellow building, to hear David Parks sing, and give his testimony. He spoke about on his first visit to Medjugorje, he was healed from Crohn's disease. Crohn's disease is an inflammatory of the bowel, which causes diarrhoea, raped weight loss and severe abdominal pain. David spoke about how the Lord chose him to do Our Lady's work, as a pilgrim guide for Marian pilgrimages in Medjugorje.

Once again Patricia sang beautifully along with David's tranquil and healing voice. Tears streamed down my face, as images of my past life had raced through my mind, childhood traumas, the many fights

101

with my father, accidents, broken relationships, drunkenness, and so on. As we joined hands to sing along to "Ave Maria", I could hear Patricia callout to Jesus to heal me. *What sort of healing she was praying for me,* I wondered. Afterwards we spoke about our experiences. She spoke about the peace she had felt in her heart since arriving, and how she loved to sing. Again, I was reluctant to tell her any of my experiences. *What would my family think, if they were to learn this?*

The following morning, it was time to return to Ireland. We all said our goodbyes to our resident guide David Parks, and another female guide, and the staff at the guesthouse. It wasn't easy saying goodbye to Violeta, not knowing would I ever see her again. Even though her last words were, "will you be back to Medjugorje?" My response was that I was not sure. Her eyes filled with what seemed to be, an aching smile. She lowered her head, and said that we should leave it in Our Lady's hands, handing me a book of Our Lady's messages. We embraced, and sadly I got into the coach and we were on our way to the airport. As the coach turned the corner, I noticed she had followed behind, waving good bye. Then she wiped her eyes, lowered her head and returned to the guesthouse. I wept with loneliness and sadness as I had watched her walk away. My heart ached. *Oh God, will I ever see her again,* I prayed, resting my head against the chilled side window as tears of sadness fell.

On our flight home I reflected on the past week, and I can honestly say, that I had learned a lot about myself and my faith. And without-a-doubt I had the most fascinating time in my entire life. Now armed with the knowledge, I could live a more simple life, rather than making life difficult for myself. I reflected on the elderly lady rolling the tobacco leaves, plus Vicka's words on how she once started to pray out of habit. Now she has turned completely to prayer. In addition, how she has committed her life completely to God. Giving those fantastic words a great deal of thought, and wondered if I was lost, and if I was lost in life, could I give myself to God. What a tall order.

It was amazing the peace which overwhelmed me, and it remains to be seen will I experience this peace when returning to my regular life. I may be thinking prematurely, but I had a nagging feeling that I would never see Violeta again, as I felt I would not be able to handle additional children. Maybe so, but it is best to leave our fate in God's Hands.

Chapter Nine

Physical Healing & Tranquillity

On my arrival home, I felt peaceful and was eager to practise my faith in God, and help others who were suffering. I attended mass and confession on regular basis. Making vast quantities of money did not appeal to me any longer. Keeping life simple, and living a more tranquil life was more appealing. I fasted on bread and water, mostly on Wednesdays.

One evening, a friend of mine and her daughter came to visit. We chatted for a while. Then I sensed the most magnificent fragrance of roses. I passed comment on the glorious scent of perfume they were wearing, forgetting I had no sense of smell since my sinus operation. They both replied that neither of them was wearing any perfume. My friend said, when Our Lady is present you can smell a beautiful sent of roses. I found this to be true, since I heard it said many times while I was in Medjugorje. Soon after that, while I was flicking through the channels on TV, as I usually did, to my amazement a feature film about the visionaries of Medjugorje called "Gospa", featuring Martin Sheen, came on one of the channels. *Was this just a coincidence, or another divine intervention*? It was wonderful to see this film, and to think that I was chosen by the Blessed Mother to visit this holy land. That night I had a horrific occurrence when one of my teeth split in half. The pain was agonizing. My immediate reaction was to place my left hand to my face. I was surprised when I felt a tingling sensation rush through my hand. I was even more surprised, because it was the exact same miraculous glowing sensation when Father Jozo had prayed over me. Within an instant, the pain had completely gone. *How could this happen*? I mused. *Had I received the gift of healing from Jesus, through Saint Padre Pio, when he appeared to me at Saint James's Church? Or had God chosen me to receive the gift of healing through Father Jozo?* If so I was reluctant to share this experience with anybody.

Reflecting back on the time Patricia and I had attended a seminar at the house of prayer, organised by Breda Laffey. I was eager to return to have her pray with me. I had two full hours in a private session in prayer with her. She prayed for all curses that were put upon me by another person to be removed and placed at the foot of the cross. I was to renounce Satan and all his teachings. Then she announced I was cleansed from all demonic curses or evil spirits that may have possessed me. That night I attended mass and another seminar Life in the Spirit given by Breda.

Somehow, as time passed, my memory loss was getting poorer. Noticing I could not recall half of my day. Spending longer times in bed and lying on the couch was as much I could do most days. There was one thing I was grateful for, I still maintained the peace and tranquillity I received in Medjugorje weeks earlier. It was now mid November, and while chatting to my parents, I was knocked for six to learn my sister Patricia's reasons for taking me to Medjugorje. It was to pray to get me back together with my wife and family. Of course this would be ideal, if the circumstances for a loving marriage would be honourable. If it is God's will to have me back with my wife and family, so be it. God is in control, not me, my family nor anybody else. He will show us the way. Despite how I felt about Violeta having two daughters, my initial thoughts were this is the end of this relationship, because I was reluctant to take on additional children. It was too much responsibility, not to mind all the gossip I had listened to in the past about people I knew who were going out, or married to somebody who had children from a previous marriage or relationship. Yet again I was ashamed of what people might say, like my parents, my family, neighbours, and my own children. Would my children disown me? Or would they accept there were two other children in my life other than them.

In reading over a couple of Our Lady's messages, and to my surprise, Violeta's address was written at the back of the book she had given me. *Is this divine intervention at work here*? I marvelled. By some means could I foresee the big picture, having a future with Violeta and the girls, maybe so? Followed this, I decided to have two copies of the photo developed that was taken with her. I posted one photo to her, along with my phone number and address. I had written a simple suggestion on the back of the photo, stating, "I Would Love To Meet You Again." However, long distance relationships do not work? Were we just two ships passing in the night? Or was I looking at this through rose-tented glasses? Was this just a fantasy, or an escape away from my real responsibilities? I eagerly awaited to find out. So therefore it occurred to me, why my plans were altered to build a much larger house to accommodate a family. *Had God intervened, and chose with His intention that we be together? Is it going to be my life role to be father to Sandra and Anita?* This frustrated my mindset. Or should I invite Violeta, Sandra, and Anita into my life and home? This was a major decision I possibly may have to make, if somehow it is in our destiny that our relationship should develop.

It may be useless thinking ahead, since I had not heard from her, since I sent her the photo. Somehow Christmas came and went; there was still no contact from Violeta. No Christmas card, not even a phone call. Guess at this stage, I was relieved, and had given up hope. I choose not to write to her, deciding it was not to be, and began to let go of her completely.

Come what may, relieved from the responsibility of having to take care of her and the girls. Somehow, that empty feeling showed its ugly head once again. The new-year came and went. Therefore, to my upmost surprise, it was on the second or third week of January. Hadn't a belated Christmas/new-years card and a phone number from Violeta arrive at my house by post. She was delighted to hear from me and receive the photo. She invited me to Medjugorje to visit her and her family. Again, fear set in, *was this the right thing to do? This relationship would never work,* I felt, because we were two worlds apart. I had two children; there was no way I was going to move to her country. Yet again, I could not see

107

her and the girl's life been uprooted by leaving their family and friends behind, so what then? This had to be though through before making a decision to travel and visit her.

After three months of spinning it around in my head and praying for the right thing to do. On recollecting back to when I witnessed Saint Padre Pio in Saint James Church. *Had he directed me to Our Blessed Mother Mary, and had She directed me to Violeta, or her to me?* After mulling over this for a couple of restless weeks, it became like a tug of war, should I call her or not. In the long run, I threw in the towel and followed my instinct. I phone her. It was great to hear her voice once again. She asked if I would travel to Medjugorje and visit her. My response was to leave it in God's hands. If it was God who brought us together, then we have nothing to worry about.

Chapter Ten

Pilgrimage of Gratitude

It was on May two-thousand-four, when I decided to return to Medjugorje. In high spirits, I gladly packed my suitcase and travelled on a personal pilgrimage for three weeks, and to visit Violeta, I might add. Being determined to learn more, and keep an additional diary of my experiences. I knuckled down and purchase a book by Wayne Weible "Letters from Medjujorje", which revealed more about other pilgrim's experiences. I also purchased a booklet on conversion, and the apparitions. Although I was already a catholic, I was eager to learn more about conversion.

I sat at the Risen Christ, and read the booklet on conversion. For some it involves having a new religious experience, and identity. This means having belief in God and the blessed sacraments, or changing from one religious identity to another. Catholicism involves participation in the sacrament. The blessed sacraments bear fruit in those which are baptism, confession, penance, and communion. In general, conversion to Christian Faith primarily involves repentance from sin, and a decision to live a life that is holy and acceptable to God, through faith and the resurrection of Jesus Christ. True conversion to Christianity is a personal experience, and cannot be forced. Christians consider that conversion requires, we believe in God and his son Jesus our Saviour. We believe Jesus suffered and died in the cross for us. Most often conversion is passed from one person to another, through our heavenly God. While an individual may make such a decision privately, usually it entails being baptized and becoming a member of a denomination or church. For all Catholics, it is required that we read the Scriptures, attend mass and confession on regular basis, and to obey the Ten Commandments.

Next morning after mass, I visited the Marble Statue of the Blessed Virgin. I had a yearning to pray to Her out of gratitude, and regarding different trials and tribulations that were ongoing in my life. I was to learn that this statue is also known as the Queen of Peace. It was carved by Dino Felici from Italy.

While praying in front of the statue, I noticed the Blessed Mother smiled for a slight moment. Because I had witnessed this in the church before, I accepted this as being the norm. I was to learn, that many witnesses claim that the face of the Queen of Peace seems to change, from a straight face, to a smile. It is said that sometimes She frowns; many say this is because of Her unhappiness with our world, or most likely our own immoral personal behaviour.

Countless pilgrims who pray to the Blessed Virgin experienced changes to their life, in the form of conversion. All pilgrims are drawn to pray at the statue of Our Lady. It is here once again, we receive all graces, love, joy, and peace in our hearts. By praying to the Blessed Mother, we ask Her to bring us closer to Her Son, our saviour Jesus Christ. This is why God had sent the Blessed Mother to earth.

Later, when all morning masses were over, I went into the church to pray for my family, and friends. Saint James Church is one of the most popular churches in the world. It is run by the religious order of Franciscans. It is today the focal point and the centre of both sacrament and prayer, not only for the local congregation, but also for all pilgrims who visit Medjugorje each year. First mass of the day starts at seven-thirty, it is Croatian, followed by English mass and then in various other languages. The evening services starts with the Holy Rosary at six, followed by the international mass broadcasted in seventeen different languages, including all of the services, healing prayer, and adoration which commences with hymns. The mass and services in Medjugorje is a gift from God. Comparable to all churches, it is where God is always present. As a daily practice, we may pray for our own personal intentions and offer our prayers for our Pope, Cardinals, the poor souls in purgatory, our priests, the sick, and for peace in our world.

When we attend mass we receive God's blessing and graces. By receiving Holy Communion we receive the body of His Son Jesus Christ. Today the Church worldwide is in need of spiritual sanctuary, and needs our prayers for spiritual healing and the healing for those who suffered in the hands of our fallen priests.

People come to Medjugorje, to find themselves, to find hope and peace, and to find change in their hearts. The importance of Medjugorje is to change and heal peoples' hearts towards mankind, to find peace in our own hearts and peace in our world. To stop violence, murders, prostitution, abortions, suicides, wars, terrorism, drug addiction, alcoholism, people suffering from depression, and to heal those to live a more happier life.

There is no room for Satan in our church. Satan was created by God thousands of years ago, as one of his perfect angels. Then he became jealous of God, and became evil. His mission is to destroy God's teachings and love for mankind. He has caused more sorrow, pain, suffering, wars and death than any other individual in the entire history of the world. He delights in destruction. Satan would like to destroy every person on earth. But God is stronger and more powerful than he. We must believe that Jesus loves us and desires to save us from self destruction, and a destructive world. We must pray for our church, because our church needs, clerics and disciples to survive until eternity.

Sauntering through the grapevines, on a rather hot summers evening on my way to the Blue Cross, which is one of my favourite places to visit in Medjugorje. I made a conscious decision when I arrived that I would spend time here with Our Lady. Also my favourite, is Apparition Hill, where I visit most evenings after the evening services. And each time I would pray the rosary. I found that being alone after dark; the hill is more tranquil and sensational. Seeing the many lights across the village is divine. The first time I went to pray at the Blue Cross, at daylight, I noticed there were two blue crosses, an upper and lower. It's said the upper cross is the original location where the children first stood when they seen Our Lady. The lower blue cross was put there to provide a more tranquil place to accommodate Ivan's prayer group meeting. In the early days of the apparitions, Ivan the visionary knelt down to pray at this very spot, and this became the site of today's Blue Cross. Pilgrims experience a more peaceful atmosphere at the Blue Cross. Countless apparitions and healings have taken place there over the long history of the Medjugorje phenomenon. Many wonder how the Blue Cross became blue. It was in 1982 a member of the prayer group was building his house close by. To indicate the meeting place for Ivan's prayer group meeting, he and Ivan built a three-foot high wooden cross. Ivan decided to paint the cross. When he got to his house, the only paint he could find was blue paint. So from that time until eternity this cross will remain blue. From that time on, pilgrims started to gather at the Blue Cross.

It is said that a pilgrim who had lit some candles, set fire to the wooden cross. Following this an Italian pilgrim approached Marija and asked the visionary, if he could take home this wooden cross and replace it with a more suitable metal cross. His request was accepted. He took a sample of the original paint from the wooden cross, and in a laboratory the contents of the blue paint was duplicated to paint the new metallic Blue Cross that is there up to this day. The same Italian pilgrim built the rock structure that surrounds the cross. He brought the original burnt wooden Blue Cross to his home in Italy, so that people could pray there. It is still there today.

There have been many, many apparitions at the Blue Cross, even though it is not the most suitable outdoor place for those who are sick, and the elderly. However, this is what Medjugorje is about, no matter how sick or elderly people are, God grants those the strength to make the effort to climb the rocks and offer it up for healing and their intentions. What's more, the Blue Cross is suitable for those who are physically unable to climb Cross Mountain or Apparition Hill. It has now got wheelchair access and steps leading all the way to the Cross. All pilgrim groups meet there for prayer and the rosary. I have been at the Cross, or in close proximity to it many times, when Ivan is in Medjugorje, where his prayer group meet. Thousands of pilgrim's swarm the area hours before the apparitions begin.

Back in the time when Yugoslavia was a communist country, it is said that the police tried countless times to arrest the prayer group members on the mountains. They never accomplished this because Our Lady always protected them. She warned the people that the police were in the area. At night when traffic subsides, the joyful singing could be heard across the locality. I then prayed the Stations of the Cross on the way to the Blessed Mothers Statue at Apparition Hill. It was spectacular to see so many pilgrims climb the hill, some barefoot, some carried on stretchers, all making their way to where the Madonna first appeared.

Next day, I made my way to the foothills to climb Cross Mountain, in penance. Hence, to prayed the Holy Rosary at the Stations of the Cross, to offer up my prayers for the forgiveness of my sins, my family and the sick. It was here I prayed for God's will in my life.

Again, I was to hand my life and my will, over to the care of God, and accept all outcomes of my life. Thus, to worship and to ask for His encouragement in devotion to His teachings, through the scriptures of the holy bible. Exhausted and parched from the sweltering heat, and in need of water, I was glad when a kind Italian lady offered me one of the bottles of water she held in her hand.

It was on the 1900 anniversary of the death of Jesus on the cross, when Pope Pius X1 envisioned that a cross be put up on one of the highest mountains in Herzegovina. A holy relic of the True Cross where Jesus was crucified was presented to the parish of Medjugorje from Pope Pius, and it was built into this cross. This relic was obtained from part of the true cross that remains in the church of the Holy Cross of Jerusalem. On the cross is written: "To Jesus Christ, redeemer of the human race, as a sign of their faith, love and hope, in the remembrance of the 1900 years since the death of Jesus".

It was in 1933, the local parishioners constructed the over eight-foot high concrete cross. They raised the large cross in less than three weeks during a bitterly cold winter, carrying all the materials and equipment by hand to the sheer top of the mountain. An entry in the parish archives revealed that the parishioners performed this difficult task in order to leave to their descendants' clear and visible proof of their deep faith for Our Lord Jesus Christ. Mount Krizevac means "Mount of the Cross". It can be seen from across the vineyards at the rear of Saint James Church and surrounding areas. On September fourteenth every year, the villagers began to meet by the cross on top of the mountain for Holy Mass, to celebrate the Feast of the Triumph of the Holy Cross. It is said that under the communist government it was forbidden to have any outside religious gatherings. Yet, back then the authorities made this mass an exception every year. And up until this present day, a priest from the parish and the local people gather at the foot of the mountain at two-pm each Friday. They climb the mountain, and recite the holy rosary at each station of the Way of the Cross.

Upon completion, Our Lady has said that the Cross on Mt. Krizevac was in God's design. "Dear children, the cross was also in God's plan when you built it. These days especially, go on the mountain and pray before the cross. I need your prayers. Thank you for having responded to My call."

Almost every pilgrim who visits Medjugorje, climbs Cross Mountain at one stage or another, praying the rosary, and reflects on their lives and their relationship with God. Like all holy places across Medjugorje, healing, conversion, cleansing and peace is experienced at the foot of the cross. Our Lady speaks to us through Her messages, that it is Her desire to see pilgrims climbing both Cross Mountain and Apparition hill. Young and old, climb the mountain barefoot in sacrifice and to offer up their suffering to God. It is at the foot of the cross I confessed all of my sins to God, and to placed them at the foot of the cross. I offered up my prayers for my personal conversion and the conversion of others, whose lives are lost to the evil one. On my descent, I felt purified and blessed by the Holy Spirit. I decided it was time to meet up with Violeta at her place of work. I felt confident that I had made the right decision to meet her once again. Previous to leaving my house in Ireland, I phoned ahead to let her know the day I would arrive. Because she had no way of contacting me, she may be worried that I had not arrived at all. I had made the decision to have three days of prayer with God, before I met with her. Bearing in mind, that God serves those who stand and wait. From the moment we met, we were both glad to see each other again. I felt the chemistry between us was now much greater than when we met the first time. I guess at this early stage, we both kept our feelings towards one another close to our chests. After work she brought me to visit her family just outside the village. Meeting Sandra and Anita, for the first time, triggered an extraordinary flashback to a couple of years earlier, when I was building my house. Those two little blond-haired girls, I had visualised in my spirit, racing about the house, resembled Sandra and Anita. Same ages, same height and blond hair, they also giggled a lot and were very friendly.

Her parents, Mato and Emiljia, her younger brothers Anto, Marko and her sister Catharina and her husband Pio, welcomed me into their home with open arms. For a moment I felt like Michael Palin on one of his adventures around the world. Here I was, sitting at the coffee table in a foreign country house, sipping coffee, and exchanging delightful stories with Violeta's family, friends and neighbours. Each of them had a singular story to converse, some about the war, and loved ones they had lost.

117

Even though I could not understand a word, I was relieved Violeta could translate their stories for me. I felt rather at home with her and her family, it was as if I knew them my entire life. In addition, this gave me something to reflect on.

Before the evening services, Violeta and I spent time in personal prayer at the large cross to the right hand side of the church. An area for silent prayer is in front of the wooden cross. This is the place where all pilgrims can light candles for their loved ones who have passed on, and for their personal intentions they bring to Medjugorje. Pilgrims pray for the poor souls, and leave their burdens, sins and prayers at the foot of the Holy Cross. A seated area is devoted for silent prayer and meditations. We both prayed at the cross for God to forgive us from all of our sin. We prayed for healing and conversion, our sickness, and healing of our hearts and body. After holy mass, we attended evening adoration at the church, which was a wonderful, tranquil experience. I wept the entire hour out of gratitude and for God's love, and blessing to guide us in our relationship.

The confessional areas are to the right of Saint James' Church. By making an honest confession, we receive God's forgiveness and absolution from our sin. Confession is most important for one's cleanliness from wrong doings and immortal sin. Since my first pilgrimage, I have made it a priority to make a sincere confession once or twice a week while I am in Medjugorje, and once a month during the rest of the year. By doing this my soul is free from sin, and from Satan's control. No person is absolute from sin, including men and women of God. We must not judge the sinner, just the sin. Many, pilgrims find a life changing experience while in Medjugorje. For some they attend mass and confession there for the first time in many years. Others are brought closer to God and a devotion to the Blessed Virgin Mary. For various young people, they receive a calling from God to become nuns and priests. Our Lady said: that there is not one man in the world that doesn't need Holy Confession.

"Dear children! In the great love of God, I come to you today to lead you on the way of humility and meekness. The first station on that way, my children, is confession. Reject your arrogance and kneel down before my Son. Comprehend, my children that you have nothing and you can do nothing. The only thing that you have and that you possess is sin. Be cleansed and accept meekness and humility. My Son could have won with strength, but He chose meekness, humility and love. Follow my Son and give Me your hands so that, together, we may climb the mountain, and win. Thank you for responding to My call."

The Bronze Statue of Saint Leopold Mandić is the work of Carmelo Puzzolo from Italy. A native of Croatia, Saint Leopold is the patron saint of confessors. He was canonised on October 16th 1983. The statue was put up in 1998 in the proximity of the exterior confessionals. He is a saint for those who feel not yet ready for confession.

A Prayer to St Leopold: - We have in heaven the heart of a mother, the Virgin Mary, our Mother, who at the foot of the Cross suffered as much as possible for a human being, understands our troubles and consoles us.

Glorious words from Saint Leopold: - "Some say that I am too good. But if you come and kneel before me, isn't this sufficient proof that you want to have God's pardon. God's mercy is beyond all expectation. Be at peace; place everything on my shoulders. I will take care of it. I give my penitents only small penitents because I do the rest myself." After those influential and sacred words from Saint Leopold, I made a conscious decision to pray at his statue, and ask for his guidance in making a sincere confession. At the rear of the dome, behind the church on the way towards the cemetery, is the Luminous Mysteries. Here I take a quiet half-hour to pray the rosary. In addition, it is here thousands of pilgrims pray the rosary and offer personal prayers for their intentions.

Further on, stands the bronze and copper statue of the Risen Christ that is quite unique and is surrounded by amazing hedges and gardens. This beautiful statue is the work of a Slovenian sculptor, Andrej Ajdič and it was presented to Pope John Paul II on the occasion of his visit to Slovenia. Pope John Paul then donated it to Medjugorje. It was put up for Easter 1998 which was the idea of Father Slavko Barbaric. Since Easter 2002, a seated area was arranged around the statue for personal and group prayer of the Stations of the Cross, and for those who physically cannot climb Cross Mountain.

A mysterious tear-like oily liquid oozes from the right knee of the bronze sculpture of the Risen Christ. This phenomenon is a mystery in Medjugorje. I have stood in line with countless other pilgrims with my handkerchief in hand; to collect drops of the liquid that flows from the knee of the sculpture. Since 2003, I still have the handkerchief containing a reddish stain from the oily liquid, stored in a locker in my house, along with rocks from Apparition Hill. Many pilgrims witnessed that the oily liquid had all of a sudden turned red on their handkerchiefs. Many others say that they had witnessed their handkerchiefs filled with blood. Others have received healing after blessing themselves with the oily liquid. There have been many accounts of weeping statues, icons, and Eucharist Hosts throughout the history of the Catholic Church. The weeping statue in Akita, Japan is one example of apparitions that have been approved by the Church.

The Suffering Soul, "Little Audrey" has been in a coma like state for many years now, and pictures and statues in her room all weep an oily like substance. Bio-Chemist Bogoslaw Lipinski was sent to test the oil from the Little Audrey's room and the composition was found to be an unknown substance. Currently the weeping items in Little Audrey's room are under a Church investigation.

Mystic Maria Espanzana who passed way on August 7th 2004, suffered at times with Christ like wounds and had the ability of healing, and capability of predicting future events. The apparitions surrounding Espananza were approved paranormal.

Most recently the weeping picture of Jesus in a small home in Robstown Texas, has made news around the world. Thousands have flocked to this small humble home to see the weeping picture of Jesus. Most of all those people come away believing it is a miracle. I then went on to pray at the cemetery called "Kovačica" where Father Slavko Barbarić is laid to rest. After I started to pray, I noticed the statue of Jesus on Father Slavko's grave started to raise its hands in a 3D fashion. For a moment I thought I was hallucinating, but then a thought came to mind, to raise my hands up to God as I prayed, then it stopped. I believe this was a sign from God, for me to raise my hands to the Lord as I prayed.

Father Slavko was an imperative supporter for the six young visionaries, from the very start, right up until his death. He had died on November 24th 2000. It was after the Way of the Cross that he led in prayer on most Friday's on Mount Krizevac, for local parishioners and pilgrims. He felt a sudden pain, and rested on a rock. Still in pain, he lay down on the ground; soon he lost consciousness and gave his soul over to the Good Lord.

Here are some beautiful words and prayer from Father Slavko Barbarić who is classed as a prominent figure in Medjugorje to those who knew him, and for those who visited his burial site, on a pilgrimage.

Prayer means keeping company with God the Father, with Jesus in the Holy Spirit. It means immersing your soul in the love of God, the peace which God gives. This is the way in which we become worthy to be called children of God. This is the time when our soul is filled with God's power to fight the evil in ourselves and around us. Prayer is essential for the spiritual life, such as, food and drink provide for the physical life. This is a beautiful prayer by Father Slavko.

Together, Violeta, Sandra, Anita and I attended mass, the Blue Cross, and Apparition Hill many times to pray for Gods will and guidance. We went to see Anita perform in a school play at Mothers Village where she attended Montessori School. It was there I met Father Svet for the first time. He was the priest at the time that was taking care of the orphans at Mother's Village. After spending three glorious weeks in Medjugorje, I had learnt so much more about this Holy Land, than I did on my first visit. And there is still a great deal more to discover about the visionaries and this spectacular place. I was sad to leave, but I vowed to return in a couple of weeks.

The most amazing thing happened, soon after I arrived home, the Medjugorje Herald was delivered to my parents' house. I was shocked to see Sandra, Violeta's oldest daughter on the cover. She had made her first holy communion a couple of days after I left. *Was this another coincidence, or was it a divine intervention?* It was the very first time my mother had ordered the Herald, in which it was great to read other peoples testimonies and learn more about Medjugorje. One afternoon while in town, I had a nagging feeling to meet up with a couple of friends, especially one friend in particular who plagued my mind all day. I sensed a troublesome intuition that this woman was in some sort of distress. When I met up with her and another friend, she had conveyed to us, that she hadn't much longer to live if she did not have major heart surgery. I felt compassion for her as she wept sadly. Again, I experienced this warm glow sensation rush through my body. I felt a strong need to pray for her, so she could be healed in the name of Jesus. Why I did this, I cannot explain. The desperate need to pray for her to be healed, had overpowered me.

A couple of months had passed. I bumped into her one day in town, asking her had she the operation the heart specialist had recommended. Her eyes welled as she gladly conveyed when she went to have the operation; all scans had come up clear. She had fully recovered. Again, I felt this miraculous warm glow sensation race through my body as she spoke with delight. Now I began to believe God had chosen me to heal people in Jesus name. By those two experiences, I was convinced I had received the gift of healing in Medjugorje.

Spiritual Healer, Eddie Stones from Emmanuel House Clonfert Co Galway, was coming to Knocknacarra Church in the city. There he was due to give a healing seminar. After mass Eddie began to speak about Medjugorje, and in between his talks he would point to a certain area in the church. He then announce, somebody in the church was been healed from back and abdominal pain, brain tumours, and even cancer. Then he asked a couple I was familiar with to approach the altar. I was intrigued when he said they had come to him one year previous for him to pray for them to have a baby. They were trying for years to conceive a child, with no results. A couple of weeks later, after Eddie had prayed over them, she became pregnant. I thought this to be amazing, and with a flash I felt a needle type prodding to my left knee, the old injury which happened in the public house back in the early eighties. Then Eddie raised his hand and pointed in my direction, saying, "there is a man to my left, and one of his knees is being healed, in Jesus Name. We praise and thank you Jesus." he implored. The woman sitting next to me was well aware of the problems I had with my knee, because she listened to me time after time again, complaining of the pain. She was my mother-in-law, my children's granny. She said, "I think Eddie must be healing your knee." I was overwhelmed to hear this, to been able to walk in comfort and no more having to release my knee after locking several times a day, for almost three decades.

A specialist at the hospital confirmed years earlier that the joints on my knee had decayed badly and arthritis had set in. He advised me to have a knee replacement, which I was considering. *Was my knee healed, and was this another Miracle in my life.* Sure enough after three days, my knee began to lock once again. Disappointed, except there was one thing I failed to notice, there was no more pain. It had completely gone. At this stage I did not care about my knee locking as long as there was no pain. Unfortunately my knee got worse, locking up to nine or ten times a day. It locked while I slept, and while I walked. Any slight movement, my knee would lock, the ligaments and muscles had become slacker. My doctor sent me to the hospital where I was informed by a surgeon who x-rayed my knee that the corrosion on my bones had completely healed. "How could this be, this is a turn up for the books," he said. Smiling to myself knowing quite well, that evening at Knocknacarra Church now confirmed I did receive healing from the Good Lord through spiritual Healer Eddie Stones. The surgeon had advised me to have an operation to repair the ligaments to prevent movement to my knee. Yet, I was reluctant to do this.

Since then, every day, I would take out the book on Our lady's messages and read one. "Dear children.
I desire to talk about love, I gathered you around Me on behalf of My Son, through His will. I want My children who understand the love of My Son and follow it to live in love and hope. It is through My Son Jesus Christ, those who trust, shall be healed. Thank you for having responded to My call."

At the end of July 2004, I travelled to Medjugorje once again. I spent another three weeks there and spent a considerable amount of time getting to know Violeta and her family. I was privileged to be there for the first day of the youth festival. The youth festival is celebrated on the 31st of July until the 6th of August. Each festival has a different theme each year, all taken from the Bible. Themes such as, "faith working through love", "Lord increase our faith, "Your word is a lamp to My feet and a light to My path", etc.

It is estimated that up to forty to fifty-thousand young people travel from nearby countries, and as far and wide as America, Paraguay, Africa, Vietnam, the UK, Syria, El Salvador, China, Japan, Ireland and more than sixty countries worldwide. Up to four-hundred-fifty priests from around the world co-celebrating the evening services in the duration of the festival. All congregating in the dome area, which is a glorious sight to witness since all priests are dressed in their white ceremonial robes.

At the beginning of the celebration a group of young people from Medjugorje parish welcomes all pilgrims to their parish. Then a representative from each country introduces their own county. The programme begins each day with Morning Prayer, talks and testimonies. At noon, there is a break for pilgrims to rest. The programme then continues late afternoon with more talks and testimonies. The evening programme begins with the rosary and is followed by the international mass. This is usually followed with a holy hour of adoration of the Blessed Sacrament.

The International Choir and Orchestra involve young people from twenty countries who visit Medjugorje especially for the festival. The programme is broadcasted live by radio station 'Mir', and many other radio stations, internet portals and TV stations. The entire Youth Festival is simultaneously translated in seventeen different languages. The atmosphere is magnificent and the crowds are absolutely fantastic.

It is impressive to see so many young people and adults alike, unite in the spirit of prayer, regardless of where they have come from. It's impressive to witness so many young people in one place, and love for the Lord that unites us all. People revisit Medjugorje time and time again out of gratitude for the graces, and peace they have received in their hearts. God has a plan for us all, and by this journey to Medjugorje brings us closer to him. It is mindboggling to experience the wonderful worship by the massive crowds, waving their thousands of flags and banners, united in song during the evening service. Beautiful hymns like, "Jesus I believe in you", "Emmanuel", "Jesus We Adore You" "Alleluia" and many more favourites of Medjugorje. Those who come to this Holy Land receive the true fruits of God.

One afternoon, myself, Violeta and the girls, joined the large crowd of people, who had gathered at the dome. An American doctor came out on the altar and give his testimony. He spoke about that in his entire career as a clinical practitioner; he performed thousands of abortions. And since his first visit to Medjugorje he said the Blessed Virgin spoke to him, and said aborting babies was a mortal sin. Since then he had never performed a single abortion. He had found Jesus in faith and conversion. To add, he is now a world leading member of the Anti Abortion Campaign. The large crowd of people cheered, and clap, waving their flags and banners to praise the Lord. Next, a drug addict gave her testimony, saying most of her adult life she had been addicted to some form of drug or other. And since she visited Medjugorje on pilgrimage three years previous, she had received conversion through the Holy Spirit. She has never taken a single drug ever since. Her work now is helping people with drug dependency. She had a group of over fifty drug free addicts, mostly teenagers from America with her on pilgrimage.

An Alcoholic gave his testimony, saying he came here five years ago a broken man. He had lost his job, home, wife and family. He defended alcohol like it was his best friend. Now he is five years sober, and is a strong member of his local prayer group, and Alcoholics Anonymous. Thanks to the power of Jesus and His Blessed Mother. Others talked about how they were involved in Raki, Yoga, and other forms of new-age activities in which the church does not approve. After visiting Medjugorje they have since abstained from such activities. I was amazed to hear those testimonies, for the reason that, once again I believe we can all change our negative ways in sin, if only we trust in Gods will for us. During the week, I arranged a meeting with Father Svet. We conversed for over one hour. He reassured me that the Holy Spirit of God is within us all. We must pray. Our bodies are temples of the Holy Spirit. We keep our spirit cleansed by believing in God, and to have faith in His word by reading the scriptures. From then on, I prayed in the Holy Spirit, and the results were triumphant. I had received God's graces, blessings, love, peace and joy in my heart and spirit. What a joyful feeling to be at peace with oneself and God.

Besides meeting new friends on Apparition Hill, the Blue Cross, Cross Mountain, or the Church grounds, the restaurants around the village, play an enormous part in meeting with likeminded people. It seems almost everybody is singing from the same hymn page. Most people discuss their beliefs in the visionaries, Mother Mary and the whole importance of Medjugorje.

Where a group of people congregate, let it be in the Church, at a Shrine, or where people draw together in prayer, the Holy Spirit is present. Most people experience the presence of the Blessed Mother Mary; it is Her presence that draws them to return time after time.

One evening during the holy rosary, I witnessed the sun spin, change colour and with the Host in the centre. What an amazing experience. I now faithfully believe, God has had me witness those phenomenon's to convince me that He is present in my life, and for me to trust in Him.

The week prior I was to leave for home, we travelled with Violetas' parents to a small town in the mountains, called Busovaca, near Sarajevo, north Bosnia. This is where she and her family were originally from. Indeed driving through Mostar was a daunting experience to witness, with many buildings razed to the ground. I must add, to observe the residual from the conflict in the early nineties; was mindboggling to see such destruction. Yet it was amazing to witness people smiling and laughing, and seemed to be getting on with their lives.

Across the region, many small villages had been destroyed, and the inhabitants had never returned. Most were probably killed in the conflict. The scenery around Bosnia and beyond is fantastic, with many rivers, and the mountain region enclosed in forests. It seems timber is a vital source of an income for the Bosnian people. Some of it is exported and a lot of it is used for fire wood. I found that the Bosnian people are very polite, and welcoming. Even though, the people were friendly and the landscape was out of this world, Bosnia would not appeal to me as a place to live. I felt there was a sense of doom and gloom in the atmosphere. Perhaps this may have been because of the war. Maybe one day this may change.

Chapter Eleven

Violeta's visit to Ireland

After keeping in touch with Violeta by phone, it was in late December 2004, she and her brother Anto, came to stay with me for two months. I guess she wanted to see how things would work out between us. We had separate rooms in respect for our faith. We got on fantastic, and enjoyed each other's company, once again. It was at this stage we both declared our love for one another. Both our hearts were full of joy and happiness, just to be in each other's company. We both agreed that Mother Mary had brought us together, so therefore we should stay together. Her view was that we are in this for life, that we must remain resilient; and toughen out the hard times. *Hard times*? I mused over. Ignoring this, after she left, I could not wait for her to return, she was such fun and easy going. Anto remained on and got a job in a local garage, where he worked for two years. He is now married to a wonderful woman from Roscommon, and he works at security in a hotel.

During the summer, Violeta returned with the girls. Both our lives were complete now, and we were very happy to be together. Although we both did not favour living together for the reason that it is a sin in the eyes of God, to live with somebody and not be married in the Catholic Church. Sandra and Anita settled into school with no problem whatsoever. They became very popular among their friends. We travelled to see different parts of the country which they loved dearly. After a couple of years, Violeta and I felt very uneasy with the company Sandra was keeping; there was a lot of drinking. After all it was I who invited them to travel to Ireland to live with me. Initially, Violeta had asked me to live in Medjugorje. I wasn't prepared to leave my children and my home, so it was best they come and stay with me. Soon there were countless racial remarks made towards Violeta and the girls. Now I know what she meant by *hard time*. This responsibility lay on my shoulders. Even though I became up in arms over this, I'm not one to give in easily. Through hell and high water, I did my upmost to ignore such rude remarks, and we agreed to carry on and get married in a registry office. What's more, when my annulment comes through we both agreed that we would get married in the Catholic Church.

On the summer of 2007, the day before we left for Medjugorje, my daughter asked me to pray for her eighty-eight year old granny, (Nanna) who she loved dearly. Her granny meant the world to her, and at the time she wasn't well, and was admitted to hospital.

I sat at the marble statue of Our Lady in front of Saint James church. Then I noticed a beautiful smile on the Blessed Mothers face. I looked around to see had any other people who were there, witness this. But they were praying and did not seem to react. Then I had a facial vision of my children's granny, as clear as if she had stood in front of me. After I had received confession that evening, I conversed to Father Kevin Devine about this. Father Kevin was the resident English speaking priest at the time. He reassured me that this person needed prayers. So every day, I prayed for her to be restored to perfect health.

On my arrival home, my son and daughter sadly conveyed to me, that their Nanna had remained in hospital and she was not responding to treatment for her illness. As weeks passed, and as I worked the night shift as a taxi driver, and in close proximity to the hospital where Nanna was as a patient. I was overwhelmed by this miraculous warm glow sensation once again. It was five to midnight; a sudden feeling of grief overwhelmed me, that Nanna was dead, or dying. Tears streamed down my face as I stopped at the traffic lights. I began to pray, asking God not to take her, since my daughter, son and their mother needed her. I pleaded with God to restore her to perfect health. As we were going through a divorce and having our marriage annulled, my former-wife and my children needed her. She was the pillar of their lives.

As tears fell, the Blessed Mother appeared to me, about twenty-feet away, and floating in mid air. I was looking towards the ceiling of the car, but could not see it. Just the Blessed Mother in the darkness, with many stars illuminating the sky behind Her. She had Her hands joined as if She was praying. First I was startled, but soon the image of Saint Padre Pio came to mind, looking in the direction of Our Lady in Saint James Church. Soon I realised that the Blessed Mother appeared to me to answer my prayers. I pleaded with Her to spare granny, as she was needed.

The Blessed Mother dressed in grey, which indicates She was working, looked down upon me. She seemed stern, as I pleaded with Her for the fifth time. Then She smiled. "You are not going to take her?" I asked. She nodded Her head, as if to say, NO, with the same beautiful smile I had witnessed four-years previous. I thanked Her and slowly She faded away. Then I heard sounds of car horns, and looking in my rear-view mirror, and noticing a line of cars behind me. Then seeing the driver to my left, had a strange look on his face, as if he had seen a ghost. He must think that something strange had happened to me.

It was then I noticed the traffic lights had turned green. For a moment or two I was dazed, and eventually moved on. I pulled over to the pavement, deciding to phone my daughter. There was an echo in the background. "You are at the hospital?" I asked. She told me in a saddened voice, that the entire family were around granny's bed. The doctors decided it would be best to turn off her life support machine. The doctor said she will not last the night. She wept as she said she would never have her Nanna in her house again, and how she loved her so much. It was then I revealed to her, that granny was not going to die. She will be sitting up in her bed in the morning.

"How can you say such a thing to me, dad, since you know how much I love my granny," she cried down the phone. It was at this point she hung up. Drained from my ordeal, I somehow managed to finish my shift. Next day, I phoned my daughter to learn, that granny was sitting up in her bed, having breakfast. I wasn't surprised by this. The doctor said, it could only have been a miracle. Granny celebrated her ninetieth birthday, on the stage singing her favourite Irish song, "Danny Boy". It is now February 2016, she is now ninety-seven years old, and is still going strong.

This miracle reassures me that Our Lady is without doubt appearing to the visionaries in Medjugorje. Sadly today my daughter has very little memory of my phone call that night her granny was dying. To me it doesn't matter; the main thing is, that Jesus Christ spared the woman's life when she was mostly needed. I get great joy in helping others. It is agonising to watch others suffer in pain or in bad health, as I know how much I have suffered myself. I pray for the love of Jesus, in His name for other people I knew that their doctors diagnosed them as only having weeks to live. The most amazing thing is, most of them I have prayed for to receive healing, are still alive. Their cancer, heart problems, and many other illnesses have shrivelled up, and they have been restored to good health. Thank to Jesus our healer. Unfortunately as time passes, my depression and memory deteriorated for the worst. Once again, I decided to attend a healing service at Emanuel House Clonfert. As Eddie Stones began the healing service, I sensed a tickling sensation inside the left side of my head, where I had received the blow at the time I had the car accident. Then Eddie said, some man to my left, his brain or memory is been healed, in Jesus name. We made eye contact for a split second, and then I was overwhelmed when my mind became crystal clear. It was like the haze had lifted. Afterwards it was a wonderful feeling to recall most of my day again. I am never shocked by those miraculous healings, because now I know Jesus loves me and is now healing all the injuries and suffering I had received over the years.

It was amazing to have the exceptional opportunity to join Vicka, one of the Medjugorje visionaries for evening mass celebrated by Father Taghg Quinn PP, at Knocknacarra Church in our home town. She also had a special apparition with Our Lady on the altar. Afterwards, Vicka was amazed to see Violeta stand beside her at the altar. *It could only have been Our Lady who arranged this special accordance.*

Not every cloud has a silver lining, because after another year or two, our family situation started to take a turn for the worst. Our relationship started to go pear-shaped. Many arguments overpowered our thoughts, over Sandra and the company she kept. Violeta had become out of control out of fear for Sandra's safety, where there were older guys involved. As a result I was experiencing chest pain during this time. One evening, I decided to drive myself to the hospital to be checked out. I was glad the doctor had decided to keep me in over the weekend for some medical test, even if it was just to get away from the stresses at home. While I lay on my bed attached to a heart monitor, the police phoned me. They had Sandra and her friends at the police station. It seemed one of their friends had asked an older guy to purchase alcohol for them. And of course, they were all apprehended by security who had called the police. There was a great deal of drinking going on in approximately of our house, and I was aware that drugs were distributed as well. We had a lot of conflict over this. The intense pressure became unbearable. My neighbours had even come into my driveway while we were away, and damaged my cars and broke a window on Violeta's car. They had up-rooted some apple tries and tossed them across the driveway. Many times they entered my house, supposedly invited by Sandra. Those teenagers started to deposit alcohol bottles around my garden. At first I went out on a limb to ignore those guys. Nonetheless, when I was told by a family member, it was the same neighbour who uprooted the apple trees and exposed himself to the girls. To add, I was informed it was he who had let the air out of the tyres on my car. I retaliated and put a rock through the back window of a scrap car he had parked in his garden. With a result of my actions, I got beaten up by him and his father, the guy who had abused me as a child.

All this occurred while I was trying to protect my home and my family. While they were punching me on the ground, I could see a vision of Our Lady, with Her out stretched arms, and tears were streaming down Her face. I could feel Her warm love as each and every time they punched me, mostly to the head. I could feel my heart swell. Fearing I was getting a heart attack, I pleaded with them to stop. Also Violeta and Anita pleaded with them to stop. They ignored our plea and kept on punching me while they held me down. As they were about to walk away the guy who had sexually abused me, kicked me in the head and walked away. At first I struggled to get to my feet. And when I did the earth started to spin. I then collapsed to the ground.

Then I was taken to hospital by ambulance, where after an x-ray showed I had a number of broken ribs. There were many abrasions to my head and stomach, where I had been kicked repeatedly. In the oncoming weeks I started to get dizzy spells, and sometimes had to hold on to the walls or doorframes to maintain my balance. The police were involved. I pressed charges for being sexually abused as a child, and the damage done to my cars, and person.

This was a wakeup call, had I made the right decision to have Violeta and the girls live with me? We were living in a horrific hostile situation. I began to question our relationship, and was it Padre Pio I had witnessed in Saint James Church? Could it happen that I may be tricked by Satan? It is said that Satan disguises himself in many faces. Was I a victim of this? Or, was I been chastised by God for leaving a previous marriage? Yet again, why would Satan bring me to Medjugorje, disguise himself as Padre Pio, then take me to the Blessed Mother and the Holy Spirit, fall in love and have three wonderful people come into my life? This was all confusing. However, Violeta and I needed time to resolve those horrendous issues we were subjected to. We both were so confused; we had no idea which way to turn. There was so much mumbo jumbo, it seemed God had abandoned us, or had we abandoned God?

It was on June 2010 we decided to return once again to Medjugorje, for a couple of weeks. Whilst there, I hoped for an answer for our very uncomfortable situation back home. And as things worked out, our relationship turned for the worst, returning to Ireland as a family was most likely not going to be. Whilst strolling around the village, seeking serenity and harmony, and answers in association with my relationship with Violeta, I noticed a large sign in the laneway heading towards the Blue Cross, stating "This Is My Time". It was then I began to seriously consider the conflict I had in my entire life back home. Could I see this changing? I don't think so.

I needed guidance on this matter, so Father Kevin Devine agreed to meet with me. We met at three-pm, by the statue of Saint Leopold Mandić. Regrettably for me, he had no answers about my family situation, only that God has his ways in dealing with those people who assaulted me. He suggested I leave it in God's hands. Then he asked me do I pray the rosary each day? I was ashamed of my answer, which was, I don't prayed the rosary every day, only once a month or so. But when I'm here at Medjugorje, I pray the rosary all the time. He suggested I pray the rosary every day, and understand Our Lady's messages, past and present. "Our Lady appears to Mirjana on the second of the month. You be there to witness this", he said. "By being there at the apparition, you will have a better insight into the visitation of Our Lady". He insisted I purchase a prayer book in the church bookshop by Father Slavko Barbaric "Pray

With The Heart". This prayer book is easy to understand and how we should pray with the heart. He then had taken a slip of paper from between the pages of his Bible, and handed it to me. "This is the Twelve Commandments," he said. "I suggest you memorise them, and live by them." Then he brought me to the church bookshop to purchase a Bible. He then picked out a Bible of the New Testament. He suggested I study it on a daily basic. "Make the bible your daily prayer book", he recommended.

What a tall order. But if I had prayed in the Holy Spirit before, surely I could repeat this once again and study the bible. Knowing it was wrong to live under the same roof with somebody when not married in church. I began to consider this a great deal.

A couple of weeks had past; and while still in Medjugorje, I met with Father Terry O'Connell from Limerick, Ireland. After sharing with him what I had gone through in my past life and recent past, he asked if I would be willing in having a deliverance prayer performed in Jesus name. I would have done anything just to bring to an end the chaos in my life, and the way I felt. After explaining to me what deliverance consisted of, we arranged a meeting for him to pray through the Holy Spirit with me. Before he started the prayer, he asked if I was prepared to surrender and submit to God. I felt whatever was going to happen, had to be better than the way my life was at that particular moment. But when he asked me was I prepared to forgive those who had abused me, now this was totally different. There was no forgiveness in me for those people. I hated them with all my heart. I was determent to see the guy who sexually abused me, go to prison. He needed to be punished for abusing me.

This is a version of the deliverance prayer Father Terry had prayed with me. He started the prayer by blessing me with Holy Water, in the presence of Jesus. Then Father asked me to repeat in my mind, if I was ready to renounce the following. - Under the authority of Jesus Christ and by the power of the Holy Spirit, I renounce all contacts or any involvement with Satan, Satanism, Black Mass and Demon worship. I renounce all contacts with Witchcraft, White Magic, Black Magic, Voodoo, Dungeons & Dragons, Spirits, Black Mass, Ouija boards and other occult games. I renounce all kinds of fortune telling, tea leaf reading, coffee ground reading, palm reading, crystal balls, tarot and other card readings, all dependency on astrology, fortune telling by the iris of the eye, birth signs and horoscopes, spirit guides, pendulum swinging, and false cults. I renounce all water witching or dowsing, levitation, body-lifting, table tipping, automatic handwriting and handwriting analysis. I renounce all Psycometry (divination through objects), Geomancy, Promancy, Aeromancy, Arithmancy, Capnomancy, Rhapsodmancy, Phrenology (fortune telling by bumps on the head) and Augury that are part of fortune telling. I renounce the heresy of reincarnation and all healing groups involved in metaphysics and spiritualism. I do renounce every psychic and occult contact that I have had. I renounce all kind of hypnosis, self hypnosis under any excuse or authority. I renounce all transcendental meditation, yoga, Zen, all eastern cults and religions, mysticism, idol worship and false religions, Reiki and Yoga. I renounce every cult that denies the blood of Jesus Christ and every philosophy which denies the Divinity of the Lord Jesus and the Trinity. Lord I confess the sin of seeking from self or Satan the help that should have only come from God. I confess as sin (name all occult contacts and occult sins committed) and also those occult sins I cannot remember. I renounce all psychic heredity that I may have had and break any demonic hold and curses over myself and my family line back to Adam and Eve on both sides of my parents through the power of the blood of the Lord Jesus Christ. I renounce all literature I have ever read and studied about Satan and his beliefs, and I will destroy such books in my possession. Lord I now repent and renounce all those sins and ask you to forgive me. I renounce Satan and all his works. I count them as my enemies. I now close the door to all practices and command all such spirits to leave me in the mighty name of Jesus Christ. I renounce the Prince of Occult Sex and all the sex spirits which entered through the occult involvement, eyes, participation, transfer or by inheritance and command all of his demons to come out of the sex organs, the lips, tongue, the taste buds, throat, and mind in the name of Jesus Christ my Saviour.

Heavenly Father, I come to You in the name of the Lord Jesus Christ, I believe that he is the Son of God Who takes away the sin of all those who repent and confess him as Lord. I believe that the blood of Jesus Christ cleanses me from all sin. I claim freedom from all filth which has come through my eyes, my ears, my mind or through actual participation in sin.

In particular, I confess the following: all preoccupation with sensual desire and appetites, and indulgences of them; all longing and ardent desire for what is forbidden; all inordinate affection, all unnatural and unrestrained passions and lusts; the promoting or partaking of these which produce lewd emotion and foster sexual sin and lust. In the name of Jesus Christ, I now rebuke and loose myself and my family from any and all evil curses, fetishes, charms, love potions all psychic powers, sorcery, bewitchments, enchantments, hexes, spells, every jinx, and psychic prayers which have been put upon us, from both sides of generations of my father and mother back to Adam and Eve. I break and loose myself from any connected or related spirits from any person or persons or from any occult or psychic source. I hereby reclaim all ground that I have ever given to Satan in body, mind, soul, or in spirit. I dedicate myself to You Dear Lord, to be used for Your glory alone. I want You to control and empower every area of my life, including all my emotions; my sexual powers; that from now on, that I might be used according to Your will. I also now give to You my affections, emotions and desires, and request that they might be motivated and controlled by Your Holy Spirit. I hereby claim, total victory and freedom from all my former bondages, in Jesus Christ' name I ask. – Amen.

Then Father Terry asked was I ready to forgive all of those people who sneered me, mocked me, assaulted me, abused me, laughed at me, made fun of me, pass judgment or spat at me, criticised me, and slated my appearance. This, I was not ready to do. Then he repeated the same words over and over again. Tears streamed down my face for hate for those people, because I was not willing to forgive them. After repeating those words a couple of times, somehow I experienced the warm pines-needles sensation run through my body. Moments later I started to experience a sense of peace come over me. As he read on and asked me to repeat in my mind, that I repent any sin in my life and place myself under the Blood of Jesus for protection. Walk confidently in the freedom and victory that only Christ provides. He has done it all for me. Rejoice!!

Within one minute after Father Terry had completed the deliverance prayer, and as tears of joy ran down my face. I felt a load had lifted from my heart and mind. The peace I encountered was phenomenal. I had serenaded my pain, anxieties and conflict to God. Even though most of the above I had not practiced in my life personally, who knows what was practised in my family generations. It was then I received the Holy Spirit once again. That evening, I was drawn to Apparition Hill to give thanks. I was restored in Gods peace. On my way back from the Hill, I was drawn to a statue of Saint Michael the Ark Angel, in one of the souvenir shops. I bought it to bring it back to Ireland to protect me, my family and my home.

After due consideration, and regrettably, I was to return to Ireland without Violeta and the girls. At first this was mindboggling and devastating, because I thought our destiny was to spend the rest of our live together. Abandon hope, life was once again empty without Violeta and the girls. There was one thing for sure; I knew living in the same village with them over again, was out of the question.

For weeks I had tried my upmost to settle back into my home and village, but found it difficult. My teenage neighbours were still taunting me with their cars, racing back and forth past my house, yelling and shouting, and calling me names. I'd spend most of my time away from the village, walking around town, lost, not know what I should do. I had envisioned Our Lady many times, with her arms out-stretched welcoming me back to Medjugorje. Even if I was at a loose end, spending a great deal of time with my children was beneficial. They both knew my situation, and could tell that I was very unhappy. I had their blessings to return to Medjugorje if I desired to do so. Having to make the decision to leave my children behind, and my home was extremely difficult. There was no way I could make this decision without God's help. It was He who decides my fate, not me.

Then the Garda Officer who was conducting my case over the sexual abuse and the assault, called me. He informed me that I had no witnesses to back up my claim, to bring this guy to justice for the abuse. Reflecting back on what Father Kevin's suggested, I decided to leave it in God hand and wash my hands from the assault as well.

After two painstakingly months, with the Lord's help I decided to rent my house and pack my bags, tie up a couple of loose ends. Making the decision to travel back to Medjugorje with the probability of living there was extremely strenuous. Saying goodbye to my parents was to say the least, heartbreaking. My father was now ninety-years old, and my mum was in her mid-eighties. We cried when we said our goodbyes. I wasn't too sure when I would see them again. A parent's sadness never comes easy to see their son or daughters immigrate.

Saying goodbye to my daughter was tiring, because I love her dearly. My loving son gave me a lift to the bus station. It was painful to get into the bus, and see the pain on his face as we said our goodbyes. As I sat there and watched him drive away, remorse plagued me as to why my life has turned out this way. But I guess this is the pack of cards we have been dealt. Arriving back to Medjugorje, I met up with Violeta. She was not sure was it a good idea for me to be there, after the conflict we had in the past. Of course, true love never runs smooth; no relationship is cut and dry, or even black or white. It took time to thrash out our differences. There was a lot of different points of view, tit for tat over where we should live, work, etc. But eventually we succeeded, when the chips were down, there was no going back. We both knew we belong together. We put the past behind us, and got on with our lives. We both turned over a new leaf, and carried on with our lives.

Most evenings after the services, I loved to saunter about the church area, with rosary beads in hand, and recite the rosary in gratitude. My most favourite place is by the Luminous Mysteries, and the beautiful hedge and gardens surrounding the Risen Christ. Praying in the Holy Spirit, and to have the Holy Spirit within us, is a special gift from God. Though, missing my children a great deal, my mission was too kept in touch with them constantly, mainly by phone and Social Media. Whereas this is certainly not a substitute for being physically active in their lives, it's best to accept it for now.

Besides taking part in most of the services, mass adoration, etc. I pondered daily as to what I would do with my time, and I had a lot of it. Working in a souvenir shop, or a restaurant was out of the question, because those jobs were held over for the local inhabitations. Somehow, one specific thought came to mind each day, it was to rewrite the many drama/romance stories I had written in first drafts, years previous. I made the decision to rewrite them into novels. Therefore, download programmes from the internet on how to write a novel. Even though, I already had the outline of the stories, and when I start to write, my mind would be blank. No further ideas would unfold from my mind, so now I had a dilemma. *Had I writers block, or was writing a novel a far-fetched flight of my imagination.* Nevertheless, while I was in the Adoration Chapel, I prayed to the Good Lord to help me formulate ideas for one specific transcript I was working on. And believe it or not, ever since that moment, when I'd say a prayer to God, Jesus and Our Lady to help me write, ideas would flow from my mind onto the page. I would come up with some brilliant ideas that were not in my mind to start with. I believe this is one of the gifts I received from God. After two-year, I had completed two book, from the Jack McGuinness epic saga series. "Still Waters Run Deep", and "Lost in Paradise". Both dramatised stories are set in Ireland, and are now available at amazom.com.

Succeeding the vicious attack by my neighbours, I'd often experience slight dizzy spells. Even so, on April 2011, just as I was about to retire for the night, I felt an acute attack of nausea. Therefore, the room began to spin. About to collapse to the floor, I made a quick dash for the bed. It felt like some sort of brain seizure, followed by sever vomiting which lasted the entire night. It felt like I was levitating on the bed. Violeta had no idea what to do. When she called the doctor, he suggested we go to the Cetluk out-patients' clinic in the vicinity of Medjugorje. This was almost impossible, as I could not sit upright from the sever spinning in my head. All I could do was to hold my head and vomit. This was the worst motion sickness anybody could ever injure. It was the worst sickness of my entire life, with the room spinning like I was on a merry-go-around. Next evening, Violeta managed to get hold of my friend, Chris, who managed to track down Nurse Jane, who was a volunteer nurse with one of the charities that looked after the sick, and the elderly in the locality. They arrived at our apartment. I could not stand up-right, because of the awful spinning inside my head. I had to slide on my back, down three flights of stairs. Then I was helped onto a stretcher and wheeled into an awaiting ambulance, to take me to a hospital in Mostar. It was there, the doctors ordered to perform a brain scan and some other tests. It was then a doctor informed to me that I was having an acute attack of Vertigo, with high blood pressure, and high cholesterol.

I was then taken to the intensive care unit. I was there for six days, holding my head which helped me cope with the motional sickness. Dreading I was going to be left in this state for the rest of my entire life, and been confined to a bed, motionless. I was attached to a tube to help me go to the toilet. No food and very little water for six days. Nothing would stay in my stomach. The medication the nurses were giving me, did not help at all. The clock hanging on the wall looked like it was moving around the room. It was a living nightmare. On the sixth night at twelve thirty, I had asked the Lord to take me, that this sickness was too much for any human to injure. Pleading with God in Jesus name, praying, Jesus I love and adore you. I asked Him to either stop this spinning in my head, or please just end my life, now. Prayed an act of contrition, in the hope I would die. After pleading for the third time, I experienced the warm glow sensation running through my body, like I had in the past when I experienced healing. It was at this moment the spinning inside my head had completely stopped. It was unbelievable. I was overwhelmed with joy, and called the nurse. She was delighted with the good news.

The first couple of weeks after I was released from hospital were horrible. Even though I was grateful to the Lord for healing me, I spent over four-weeks walking around Medjugorje with two walking sticks and dark sunglasses. My head hurt a lot, sharp lights and sound created severe tension on my brain. I set for hour after hour in Saint James' church and the adoration chapel, praying for the vice-like tension to my head to go away. I could only stand upright for a short time. While in the village, I sometimes had to lie flat on the pavement, or on the benches at the rear of the church, to take the pressure from my brain. Also my left knee kept locking, in which it was very uncomfortable.

After almost two months, the tension in my head subsided. What a relief. A normal life seemed possible once again. I discovered through Doctor Mehmet Oz, from DoctorOz.com. Who is an American Cardiac Surgeon and Host of the Dr. Oz TV. He was adamant that coffee, and epically caffeine, activated the tension and dizziness if one suffers from vertigo. Moving ones head from side to side; also prevent dizziness, or vertigo attacks. The doctor advised me at the hospital, not to fly for at least one year. I needed to get back to Ireland. So in the beginning of June, I booked my flight for the 28th of August, of that year, or so I thought. It turned out that I had mistakenly booked my flight for the 24th of June, which was two weeks later. I was full of fear of flying. My Medjugorje friends told me that I was going back to Ireland on that date, for some particular reason.

I was surprised to discover, that on the same day I arrived back home at my parent's house, my father was admitted to hospital. This saddened me, as I wanted to spend time with him. I was also looking forward in spending time with my son and daughter once again. The first time I visited my father at the hospital, he wept for a moment. I was overjoyed to witness this; because this reassured me he was glad I was home and came to visit him. My annulment was approved, and I was free to marry in the Catholic Church. Also a letter arrived at my house for me to have an operation on my left knee, to repair the damaged ligaments and cartilage. My doctor had made this appointment two years previous. It was best to postpone this appointment for a couple of months. I also had other health problems, such as high cholesterol, high blood pressure and chest pain. I was admitted to the same hospital as my father for one day medical tests. It turned out my medical symptoms weren't life threatening. My father was now two-months in hospital, which did not look good for him. One morning, I had just woken up at approximately seven-thirty; there was a noise in my mother's bedroom. I thought she might have gone to the toilet, and I did not bother to check on her, since she always managed on her own. Hours later when I entered her bedroom, she was sprawled out on the floor. She complained of having chest pain and within a half hour or so, my sister-n-law and I, had got her to the hospital. At the hospital the doctor's conveyed to us, that our mother had a slight heart attack, which had caused her to fall. I had no idea that noise I heard in her bedroom was her falling against the radiator. So not alone was my father in hospital, so was my mum. It was a stressful time for my entire family.

Two weeks later, my father had slipped into a coma. The entire family took turns on a day and night vigil. So I decided to go to the hospital at nine-am to relive my sister-in-law who stayed with my father through-out the night. I sat beside his bedside, reflecting on the good times I had with him throughout our lives. I was so grateful we had become friends, tears streamed down my face. I reflected on the first time I had huge him, it was an amazing feeling. When I turned to chat to him, I noticed he had stopped breathing. At this moment, I felt he had gone to the Lord. It was a sad moment, but I was privileged to have been there at his death-bed in his last moments of his life. I sat with him for a silent ten minutes before notifying the nurses.

Two days later we bid our last farewell to our father. My mum returned home from hospital. At this stage it was time for me to return to Medjugorje. It never gets any easier saying goodbye to my children, my mother, family, and friends. But deep down, living in Medjugorje, it is the best place for me, Violeta and the girls.

Chapter Twelve

Healing at the Risen Christ

Within a couple of weeks, I fitted into my life in Medjugorje. Despite living in one of the smallest bedsits known to man, with not enough room to swing a cat, it didn't matter, as long as Violeta and I were together. And to add, we were actually living in one the most beautiful and tranquil places on earth. Once again, I became sick and tired of my left knee locking, which caused me a great deal of discomfort. I prayed in front of the tabernacle at Saint James' Church for healing. What's more, I attended several healing prayers services, and blessing after the international mass. One evening, I pleaded to God for healing on my knee, as I did not want to have the major operation. I walked to the Risen Christ after saying the Holy Rosary at the Luminous Mysteries. I prayed at the Risen Christ, and then placed my hand on the weeping knee. Instantly I felt my knee improve, and it felt more taut and stronger. This was amazing, from that moment on, my knee has never locked or caused me any discomfort. It is completely healed. I have walked on rocks, uneven surfaces, and no locking whatsoever. Praise to the Lord.

It was February two-thousand-twelve, that there was a snow blizzard across Bosnia and Herzegovina, covering Medjugorje in almost a meter of snow. One evening, while making my way across the dense show to the Adoration Chapel before five-pm as it closed by then.

I noticed a large Alsatian type dog scurrying across the snow, heading my way. Fortunately for me the dog was running twice as fast as I was. I was doing my upmost to get away from him, before he caught up with me. The snow was so deep; it was almost imposable to drag my feet along. Soon the dog caught up with me, knocking me over and started to lick my face. Of course this gentle giant was a family pet and was very friendly. As I was about to position my foot under me to stand, I felt a snap or cracking sound on my left hip. *Here we go again, will I be ever free from pain.* Making my way to the Adoration Chapel, I limped a little and felt a slight pain to my left hip. Next morning I woke up to the most scrutinizing pain. My left knee was the size of a football. I went to the doctor; he could do very little for me, only to advise me to go the hospital in Mostar for an x-ray. He gave me a prescription for painkillers. I decided to give the hospital a miss, as I was going back to Ireland in a couple of months.

Three months later, after spending almost the same amount of time confined to the bed and couch, because my left knee was so swollen I could not walk. I had developed sinus sinuses, back and neck pain. Gaining almost two and half stone in weight, and I felt terrible. Determined I had enough, I decided to turn to prayer for healing. Making my way to Saint James church, I sat in the same seat where I sat on my first visit in two-thousand-three. I began to say the Rosary and half way through I was in so much pain, I rested my head on the seat in front for a moment to gather my thoughts. It was then I decided to yell at God from within, to take away this hideous pain, because I cannot take any more. I made a deal with him; if he wasn't going to take away my pain, then take me as I have enough. I looked back on my life of pain and distress, and could not take any more. I felt I'd rather be dead that to live with this pain on my knee, back, neck, headaches and sinuses. Somehow, I managed to finish the Rosary and had a quiet moment with Our Lady before the Holy Rosary and evening Mass.

After mass, I was about to return home, and then I had a burning desire to go to the Resin Christ Statue. Dragging my left leg behind me in a struggling pain, I somehow managed to get there with nobody about but myself. I had a moment with the Lord before taking the Weeping Tears from the knee, and rubbing it on my back, neck, hip, knee, and forehead. Within an incants, the pain on my neck had vanished. I was so amazed with this; I rubbed on the Weeping Tears, for the second time. By the time I got home, most pains that I was experiencing were completely gone. Now I was still left with a swollen knee and still in horrific pain. I went to the Church again next day, sat in the same seat and asked Jesus why heal the other pain and not my knee and hip. Inside my spirit, I could see Jesus and Mother Mary smile.

Next morning while watching a program on the television, called "In Good Health", a doctor who spoke in German, in which I could not understand a word. He pointed a wooden pointer at a red blotch on the hip and knee of a model of a human carcass. I guessed this meant an inflamed area. Then a male voiceover explained in English that a damaged tendon or ligament to the hip can cause inflammation to the knee and swelling. Surgery was the only answer for this complaint.

I lay on the couch, and began to place my finger on the injured area on my hip. I felt knotted tissue moving about. I massaged it with my fingers, then suddenly the knotted tissue disappeared. I thought this was peculiar, until I stood on my feet. The pain was completely gone on my knee. I couldn't believe I could walk about once again with no pain what-so-ever on my knee or hip. It had taken another three-month, or more to free out my knee with self psychotherapy as it was completely stiff, because I had not bent or straightened it in over three months. After these experiences, I now firmly believe, God helps those who help themselves. What's more, I believe it is my faith in God, that I received those miraculous healings in Jesus name.

I am at my best when I enter the grounds of Saint James's church. It is so peaceful to sit at the Statue of Our Lady, to the main entrance. There is one thing about this particular statue that continuously occurs as I'm about to pray. Her facial expression seems to change from time to time. Sometimes Mother Mary has a beautiful smile, and of course she has a disapproval frown, as if She does not approve of my sometimes negative attitude or behaviour. And of course Her beautiful smile tells me She is glad to see me visit Her to pray. Now some people might add, this is all in one's mind, to experience this phenomenon. It occurs each time I pray at this specific statue. Not alone that, Her left hand appears to rise almost like a 3D effect, this is an indication to me to raise my hands to the Lord as I pray.

From time to time, I still see the sun spin, with the Host in the centre. And nowhere else in my travels have I witnessed this. Other people conveyed to me that they had experienced the exact same thing and enlightened me that this was not all in one's head. It was Our Lady's way to let us know she is present. Attending mass in Medjugorje is still a special experience for me. And also to attend adoration which commences with hymns sung by the beautiful, and tranquil singing voice of Italian church vocalist, Roland Patzleiner.

For some people, being a good Christian means living a good Christian life, like not causing any hurt or pain to another person. Some people's beliefs are, if they are respectful and loyal to our priests and the Church, they will most likely get into heaven. Others attend mass, and confession on a regular basis. They help keep the church maintained. They feel by doing all of this good work, it's honouring their faith. This is not necessary the case. Because despite this, some fight with their family, neighbours, gossip, and spread vicious rumours about people, and judge others. Remember, Satan love this. This is not the Christian way. God hates gossip, he condemns those who gossip and judge others. We are all God's children. The Good Lord expects us to live our lives by the scriptures. We must constantly pray, because prayer is a one-way conversation between you and God.

Each and every one of us has a claim to some sort of possession, in the form of wealth, properties, motor vehicles, etc. We can even claim ownership to power, control, leadership, and people. But it can all be taken away from us in an instant. However, there is one thing in life nobody can take away from us, that is our life experiences. It is the only thing we as people will take with us when we leave this earth. From the moment we are born, we start to experience, things all around us. The first face or in shadow form a baby sees is their mother. We must honour our mother. Our Blessed Mother is Mother of all mothers.

Throughout my life I have had many experiences, such as joy, pain, sadness, wealth, poverty, travel, meeting wonderful people, and those who are not so wonderful. In addition I appreciate Gods creations in remarkable landscapes, such as coastal sceneries, mountain landscape, fabulous beaches, etc. But the greatest experience of all was my visit to Medjugorje, it is the most tranquil and peaceful place on earth. I believe those who wish to change their lives for reasons known to themselves, should travel on pilgrimage to Medjugorje.

Violeta and I have finally decided to get married in the church in the summer of two-thousand-sixteen. We decided to work on Violeta's house in Busovaca north Bosnia, a house that she and her previous husband had built. We planned to live there for the winter months. My daughter now lives in Melbourne Australian, where she works as a psychiatric nurse. My son is Co Owner in a security firm in Galway Ireland. Sandra is now twenty-two, and is working at the BMW factory in Munich Germany. She hopes to pursue her career as a psycho-therapist, in which she studied and qualified for while in school. Anita lives with us, and is studying hairdressing and beauty cosmetics. One day she hopes to open her own beauty salon.

Over the years from time to time, I would hear miracle stories about Lourdes in France, and Knock Shrine in the west of Ireland one hour from where I lived. At Knock Shrine county Mayo Ireland, it was the evening of the 21st August 1879, at about eight-pm, fifteen people, whose ages ranged from five years to seventy-five and included men, women, teenagers and children. They witnessed what they claimed was an apparition of Our Lady. Also appearing beside Her was, Angles, Saint Joseph, and Saint John the Evangelist, at the south gable end of the local small parish church, the Church of Saint John the Baptist.

At Knock Shrine, many people were, and still are cured of cancer and other illness. Along with people who were confined to wheelchairs, were miraculously cured and began to walk again. Many young women who had visited Knock Shrine received a calling to serve Jesus to become nuns, along with young men receive calling to serve Jesus in priesthood.

In 1858, Our Lady appeared to a peasant girl called Bernadette Soubirous at Lourdes in south-western France. Bernadette was then later canonized. It is witnessed that thousands of pilgrims have been cured from all sorts of illnesses while on pilgrimage to Lourdes.

I first started to write this book "Witness to Medjugorje", in 2012. Since then I was reluctant to share my testimony with the world. I was guided by the Blessed Mother to share my experiences with selective friends and pilgrims I met in Medjugorje. But I failed to write my story. Fear overpowered me.

In 2015 I made several failed attempt to open up, and write some vital personal experiences about my life. On January 1st 2016, I read a post on twitter about a friend of Medjugorje, Mary McCarthy from Ontario Canada. She was a Witness to the Holy Spirit in Fire. Now she is ready to share her story to the world. From the moment we became friends also on Social Media. I asked her to pray for me for courage to write my story. And so she did. With her help and the grace of God, Jesus and the Blessed Mother, I have completed my testimony. Then Mary asked me to pray for healing on her spine. She had a medical condition called Spinal Stenosis, in which I had no idea what this was. She was experiencing a lot of pain. As I read her message, I had this miraculous warm glowing sensation rush through my body once again. For the first time, two grey glowing circles appeared directly in front of my left eye in mid air. At first I thought I was going to get a stroke, or a heart attack, until I counted twelve golden glowing stars between the circles. This indicated to me that Our Lady was present, because it is reported by the visionaries; She wears a crown of twelve golden stars. At once I was compelled to pray for healing in Jesus Name, for Mary's spine to me healed. I sent her a message of an exercise on how to release pinched nerves on her lower back, because the Lord had shown them to me. I could see soft tissue trapped between the discs. She carried out the exercises, and confirmed the next day that the pain in her back was complete gone. Which means the Spinal Stensois is now completely healed. Praise to the Lord.

There is no greater way to gain knowledge and be drawn into a deeper understanding of Jesus' life than praying the rosary. It is phenomenal the amount of graces that we receive as a result of praying the holy rosary. Our Lady asks, that we pray all decades of the rosary every day. She asks that every family pray the rosary as a family together as well as reading a small passage from the bible every day. A family that prays together stays together.

Chapter Thirteen

Physical Health & Wellbeing

After my horrible experience with vertigo, and a spate of bad health, I had a yearning to maintain a healthier life. I have read many books on human wellbeing, and health issues. Back in 2007 while in Galway, I attended a collage introduction course on physiotherapy at G.M.I.T. I have read many books on physiotherapy, and attended many twelve step groups on addiction, along with group therapy, on obsessive behaviour therapy.

This helped me greatly to stop drinking and quit smoking. On the other hand, I became addicted to caffeine. After a couple of years drinking six to eight cups of coffee a day, it took its toll on my body. Aches and pains had taken over. But after a visit to my G.P, I explained to her how I felt. She advised me to change my diet. The first thing I tried to accomplish was to take care of my physical health. When I learnt about the effects of caffeine through the U.S. food and drug administration (FDA), I felt it was time to cut down on my coffee intake. I had a yearning to learn more. Not knowing that caffeine is a naturally occurring substance found in many plants, including coffee beans, kola nuts, cacao pods and tea leaves. Caffeine can also be man-made, and it is added to many of our foods and drinks. Many over-the-counter and prescription medications contain caffeine. It is a stimulant which aids fat burning and can improve exercise performance. Caffeine is also a central nervous system stimulant. It can temporarily keep you awake and make the body more energetic. However, it can also give you the jitters, shakes and headaches, this is known as withdrawals. The harmful effects from caffeine are irritation and migraine. It gives you heartburn, causes nausea and vomiting, and increases blood pressure. Caffeine in large amounts may interfere with absorption and metabolism of calcium. This can contribute to bone thinning (osteoporosis).

Caffeine causes a build up of inflammation in the bones and muscles, which causes stiffness and soreness. It causes confusion, increased urination, diarrhoea, rapid heartbeat, muscle aches. Caffeine raises the amount of acid in your stomach and may cause heartburn or upset stomach, like acid reflux or ulcers. In the reproductive system, caffeine can cause your baby's heart rate to increase. Too much caffeine can also cause slowed foetal growth and increase risk of miscarriage. In most cases, a little caffeine is safe during pregnancy. If you have an anxiety disorder or sleep disorder, caffeine may make it worse.

According to the U.S. food and drug administration about ninety-percent of the world's population ingests some form of caffeine every day. It is safe for most healthy adults to consume up to four-hundred milligrams of caffeine per day. Six-hundred milligrams a day is generally considered too much, which is the equivalent of four to seven cups of coffee. It is safe to consume two average coups of coffee each day. But if you eliminate caffeine from your diet, your body will benefit greatly, without doubt, leaving you to live a most relaxed and a healthier life.

Drug and Alcohol Related Issues

According to the U.S. food and drug administration overdosing on alcohol can seriously damage your health and can lead to death. Alcohol is a depressant because it slows down the functions of the central nervous system. This means that normal brain function is delayed, and a person is unable to perform normally. Alcohol also affects a person's information processing skills, also known as cognitive skills, and hand-eye coordination, also referred to as psychomotor skills.

Below are a number of signs to indicate if you have a drink problem? Read those vital signs, and if you can answer up to half of those questionnaires, this means you may be on your way to becoming an alcoholic, and develop alcoholism.

Alcoholism is an alcohol dependence syndrome. It is a broad term for drinking that results in problems, be it in life situations, health, or mental health problems. If your answer all of the questions, this means you are now an active alcoholic. - When disappointed, do you drink heavily, under pressure, sad, stressed, or when you have had an argument with someone? - When drinking with friends or other people, do you try to have a few extra drinks making sure that they won't know about it? – Is your intake of alcohol now, much greater than when you first started to drink? - Do you avoid family or close friends while you are drinking? - Have you ever been unable to remember part of the previous evening, even though your friends say you didn't pass out? - Do you sometimes feel uncomfortable if alcohol is not available?

-Are you more in a hurry to get your first drink of the day than you used to be? - Do you sometimes feel a little guilty about your drinking? - Has a family member or close friend expressed concern or complained about your drinking? - Have you been having more memory blackouts recently? - Do you often want to continue drinking after your friends say they've had enough? - Do you usually have a reason for the occasions when you drink heavily? - When you are sober, do you sometimes regret things you did or said while drinking? - Have you tried switching brands or drinks, or following different plans to control your drinking?

-Have you sometimes failed to keep promises you made to yourself about controlling or cutting down on your drinking? - Have you ever had a drink driving conviction, or any other legal problem related to your drinking? - Are you having more financial, work, school, and/or family problems as a result of your drinking? - Has your physician ever advised you to cut down on your drinking? - Do you eat very little or irregularly during the periods when you are drinking? - Do you sometimes have the shakes in the morning and find that it helps to have a little drink, tranquilizer or medication of some kind? - Have you recently noticed that you can't drink as much as you used to? - Do you sometimes stay drunk for several days at a time? - After periods of drinking, do you sometimes see or hear things that isn't there? - Have you ever gone to anyone for help about your drinking? - Do you ever feel depressed or anxious before, during or after periods of heavy drinking? – Does any of your blood relatives have a problem with alcohol, now or in the past?

Now that you have read the questionnaire, it is up to you to decide whether you are an Alcoholic or not, or if you want to quit or not. Now take a moment to read the effects alcohol can cause to the human body. - Slurred speech, drowsiness, upset stomach, vomiting, diarrhoea, headaches, breathing difficulties, distorted vision and hearing. It impaired judgment, decreased perception and coordination, unconsciousness, anaemia which is loss of red blood cells, this means lack of iron in the blood. Do you suffer from paranoia, blackouts, this means memory lapses. This is when you cannot recall or remember events that take place while you were under the influence of drugs or alcohol.

Terrifying eh, well keep on reading and discover the long-term effects which are associated with many health problems which large amounts of alcohol can cause. - Unintentional injuries, such as car crash, falls, burns, drowning, firearm injuries, sexual assault, domestic violence, increased on-the-job injuries, and loss of productivity. Increased family problems, violence, and broken relationships. Alcohol poisoning, high blood pressure, stroke, and other heart-related diseases, liver disease, nerve damage, sexual problems, permanent damage to the brain, vitamin B1 deficiency, which can lead to a disorder characterized by amnesia, apathy and disorientation. It causes ulcers, gastritis which is an inflammation of stomach walls, malnutrition, causing cancer of the stomach, mouth and throat.

Did you know that over two million people suffer some sort of physical condition from alcohol related injuries worldwide each year. On average, two out of three people will be involved in a drunken driving accident some time in their lifetime. Alcohol and drugs impairs concentration, comprehension, coordination, vision, and reaction time. Being convicted of driving under the influence of drugs or alcohol can impact your life in ways you may not be aware of, including loss of employment, prevention of employment in certain jobs, higher insurance rates, serious financial setbacks, and personal embarrassment.

When misused, prescription drugs, over-the-counter drugs, and illegal drugs can impair perception, judgment, motor skills, and memory. Remember, all drugs are chemicals, and because of their chemical structures, they can affect the body in many different ways. In fact, some drugs can even change a person's body and brain in ways that last long after the person has stopped taking drugs, maybe even permanently. Dopamine is a neurotransmitter present in regions of the brain that regulate movement, emotion, awareness, motivation, and feelings of pleasure. When drugs enter the brain, they can actually change how the brain performs. These changes are what lead to compulsive drug use, and addiction.

Abusing drugs, such as nicotine, cocaine, marijuana, ecstasy and heroin etc, leads to all sorts of illnesses and disabilities. People who live with substance dependence have a higher risk of all bad outcomes including unintentional injuries, accidents, risk of domestic violence, medical problems, and death. The impact of drug abuse and dependence can be far-reaching, affecting almost every organ in the human body. Drug use can weaken the immune system, increasing susceptibility to infections. Cause cardiovascular conditions ranging from abnormal heart rate to heart attacks. Injected drugs can also lead to collapsed veins and infections of the blood vessels and heart valves. It causes nausea, vomiting and abdominal pain. Sharing needles can transmit the HIV virus from one person to another.

It is a no brainer for one to realise, those illegal drugs can cause the liver to have to work harder, possibly causing significant damage or liver failure. A person can have seizures, stroke and widespread brain damage that can impact all aspects of daily life by causing problems with memory, attention and decision-making, including sustained mental confusion and permanent brain damage along with extreme paranoia. Many drugs have been shown to alter the brain chemistry, which interferes with an individual's ability to make decisions and can lead to compulsive craving, seeking and use, which leads to substance dependency. All drugs such as nicotine, cocaine, marijuana, ecstasy etc, give the drug user a false high. The reward for taking such drugs leads to dopamine. This is what causes the "high" or euphoria associated with drug abuse. There is a high price to pay for those unnatural highs and euphoria, such as behavioural problems, paranoia, aggressiveness, hallucinations, addiction, impaired judgment, impulsiveness, loss of self-control and birth defects. Nearly four percent of pregnant women in the United States alone use illicit drugs such as marijuana, crack cocaine, ecstasy, heroin and other amphetamines. These and other illegal drugs may pose various risks for pregnant women and their babies. Some of these drugs can cause a baby to be born too small or too soon, or to have withdrawal symptoms, birth defects or learning and behavioural problems.

Additionally, illegal drugs may be prepared with impurities that may be harmful to a pregnancy. Pregnant women who use illicit drugs may engage in other unhealthy behaviours that places their pregnancy at risk, such as having extremely poor nutrition or developing sexually transmitted infections. Alcohol and drug addiction has a profound negative effect to our health systems worldwide, eating into public funds, costing the tax payer multibillions annually.

Sobriety and Recovery

It is estimated that over twenty million people are in recovery from addiction in the United States alone. Alcoholics Anonymous (AA) is now a worldwide fellowship. It was founded in 1935 by Bill Wilson and Doctor Bob Smith in Akron Ohio. Alcoholics Anonymous states that its primary purpose is to help alcoholics to achieve sobriety and help alcoholics recover from alcoholism. With other early members Bill Wilson and Bob Smith developed AA's Twelve Step program, for spiritual and character development. With the Grace of God and the twelve step programme, there are millions of men and women clean and sober through Alcoholics Anonymous and Narcotics Anonymous worldwide. When people make their minds up to quit alcohol and drugs, they already start to feel good, and they begin to feel they could have a great life ahead to benefit from. It is then the recovery starts, and the longer they maintain their sobriety, the more reasons they will have to feel even more excited about life. Recovery opens up a new world of hope and opportunity. Free from the physical/mental addiction, sickness and devastation from drugs and alcohol. Once people put their addiction behind them, they are sure to have some great days ahead. No more slavery to the demon drug.

At first, some may feel that their lives are over. They feel they will never have fun ever again. This sort of negative thought crosses the minds of many newcomers as they take their first tentative steps in recovery. How wrong they are. For most addicts have survived a near-fatal brush with alcohol or drugs, almost ending in death. It is after those horrific experiences, people insist on enjoying life. Living one day at a time, staying focused in a positive way of life. Those who choose to join Alcohol Anonymous and Narcotics Anonymous have the experience of long time members before them. It is those long time members who act as sponsors, and with the help of God, they take the newcomer under their wing to help them achieve sobriety.

Of course staying clean and sober is hard work, but it is well worth it. Being drunk and high is unnatural. Discovering natural highs without drug and alcohol is the best euphoria of all. Clean and sober addicts become part of their communities in which they live. They become the best they could be as fathers, mothers, brothers, sisters, and friends in our society. Nowadays there are many drug and alcohol treatment centres worldwide. Those who chose to fall off the wagon, make a conscious decision to do so. They feel that sobriety is not for them, the addiction seems to be greater than the will to stay clean and sober. Nevertheless, if those addicts do not die, but instead hit rock bottom and decide to quit, it is then and only then their sobriety begins. There can be light at the end of the tunnel for every addict, that treatment works and that people can recover and live productive lives. The addict must be willing to stop. Imagine waking up morning after morning and not feeling the urge to use or drink. This is the best gift an addict receives after they quit.

One day at a time, recovery offers a way to turn the pain into progress. Social connections are important in recovery. Throughout the recovery community, such as AA and treatment centres, there are gatherings of all sorts where people in recovery and their family members and friends can relax in a clean and sober social atmosphere and enjoy each other's company. Today, people are making substantial progress from active addiction through treatment centres worldwide. Such centres helps the addicts address their emotional or mental health problems, improved family relationships, and helped them plan for the future. Alcoholics share their experiences, strength and hope with each other to maintain their sobriety. They have a profound compassion for those who are still suffering. Remember, being grateful is the key to lifetime sobriety. If you are desperate to change your ways, your attitude to life, people, places and things, seek professional help. Most drug and alcohol treatment centres found that the "Just for today" card can help their patients meditate, and add those words of wisdom into their daily activities and thinking.

Just for today, I will try to live through this day only, and not try to tackle my whole life problem at once. I can do something for twelve hours that would appeal to me if I felt that I had to keep it up for a lifetime. - Just for today, I will be happy. This assumes to be true what Abraham Lincoln said, that "most folks are as happy as they make up their minds to be." - Just for today, I will try to strengthen my mind. I will study. I will learn something useful. I will not be a mental loafer. I will read something every day that requires effort, thought and concentration. - Just for today, I will adjust myself to what is, and not try to adjust everything to my own desires. I will take my "luck" as it comes, and fit myself to it. - Just for today, I will exercise my soul in three ways: I will do somebody a good turn, and not get found out. I will do at least two things I don't want to. - Just for exercise. I will not show anyone that my feelings are hurt; they may be hurt, but today I will not show it. - Just for today, I will be agreeable. I will look as well as I can, dress becomingly, talk low, act courteously, criticize not one bit, not find fault with anything and not try to improve or regulate anybody except myself. - Just for today, I will have a program. I may not follow it exactly, but I will have it. I will save myself from two pests: hurry and indecision. - Just for today, I will have a quiet half hour all by myself, and relax. During this half hour, sometime, I will try to get a better perspective of my life. - Just for today, I will be unafraid. Especially I will not be afraid to enjoy what is beautiful, and to believe, that I give to the world, so the world will give to me. The Serenity Prayer can be most beneficial in accepting the things we cannot change. - "God grant me the serenity to accept the things I cannot change, the courage to change the things I can, and the wisdom to know the difference."Remember if we cannot change people, places or things, it is by acceptance we find the most serenity. There is good and bad in everybody, so who am I to judge God's creations. Do three things each day you would normally put off.

Prayer for healing

May the flame of my prayer rise to heaven, like incense on the wind. May the Angels and all the Saints in Gods Heaven hear our prayers and circle round in wisdom and love. Amen.

Prayer to Saint Jude for Healing

Most holy Apostle, Saint Jude, I place myself in your care. Pray for me; help me remember that I am not alone in my struggles. Please join me in asking God to send me hope in my sorrow, courage in my fear, and healing in the midst of my challenges. Please ask our loving God to fill me with the grace to accept whatever my life holds and to strengthen my faith in His healing power. Thank you, Saint Jude, for the promise of hope you hold to all who believe, and inspire me to give this gift of hope to others. Amen.

Sustaining a more Healthier Life

There are vital steps we must follow religiously. A healthy diet is imperative to maintain a strong and healthier body. Doctor Oz and countless other medical doctors maintain, people who eat a serving of fresh vegetables, fruit, nuts, and berries daily, have a thirty-two percent lower risk of having a heart attack. Our bodies benefit more from the flavonoids in berries known as anthocyanins, which act as an antioxidant. This gives the fruits their red and purple colours. Anthocyanins are known to benefit the endothelial lining of the circulatory system, which prevents plaque from building up in the arteries as well as helping to reduce blood pressure.

Fruit can be immensely beneficial to our health, as it's a natural source of vitamins, fibre, and antioxidants. Did you know that fruits also contain fructose which is a fruit sugar that is harmful to your health if consumed in excess. All fruits must be consumed in moderation, especially for those who are overweight or suffer from high cholesterol, or heart disease. Berries are among the healthiest fruits a person can eat, such as strawberries, raspberries, blackberries, blueberries, cherries, along with coconuts, avocados, pomegranate, pineapple and kiwi. All those fruits work as antioxidants inside the body, breaking down harmful fats and toxins in the blood which passes through the digestive system. Berries and bananas also improve memory loss and concentration, along with fresh fish, plus omega three, six and nine. The liver is one of the largest organs in the body. It has many important functions. Its main function is to convert the nutrients in our diets into substances that the body can use. The liver stores these materials, and supplies the body's vital cells with those nutrients when needed. It also collects toxic substances such as harmful fats, and converts them into harmless materials, making sure they are released from the body. Blood that comes from the digestive organs flows through the portal vein to the liver. In addition, it carries nutrients, medication, and also toxic substances. Once they reach the liver, these substances are processed, stored, then altered and detoxified, passing back into the blood or released into the bowel to be eliminated. The liver can also remove alcohol from your blood and get rid of by-products from the breakdown of medications. Oats porridge collects unwanted fats, sugars and deposits them through the bowel to be eliminated from harming the body.

Also, many teas act as an antioxidant; mainly green tea is the most effective. It is loaded with antioxidants and various substances that are beneficial for health, eliminating inflammation from the bones and various parts of the body. Studies have shown that green tea can decrease fat, and help to lose body weight. The bioactive substances in the tea leaves dissolves in boiled water and make it effective and obtains a response from healthier living tissue. A cup of green tea contains much less caffeine, than a cup of coffee, but still enough to have a mild effect. Green tea is loaded with potent anti-oxidants called catechins, a substance that can boost ones metabolism that can sustain chemical transformations within the cells of living organisms.

Back pain – most of us who suffer from lower back pain, without injury, is most likely caused by pinched or trapped nerves. At least eighty-percent of us suffer from some sort of back pain. Trapped nerves are most likely caused by posture, un-supportive seating and mattress. A memory foam mattress is recommended to support your back as you sleep. While sitting, use a cushion to support your lower back. The most excellent way to release trapped nerves is stretching exercises. A simple task involves laying on a flat surface, simply bend your knees close to your chest and hold, move your lower back from side to side to release those trapped nerves. Repeat this exercise first thing in the morning, and immediately when you feel lower back pain. Remember, green teas, and omega three, six and nine, fresh fruit and vegetables, fights inflammation, keeping those bone joints oiled for a more active and pain free life.

Depression and Natural Remedies

It is hard to comprehend that mental illness and depression has a profound impact on over one-hundred-million people worldwide. Yet, it is such a stigmatised illness that those who suffer from it are looked down upon by those who claim they do not have the illness. In fact most of us suffer from depression and we are not even aware of it.

Here is a list of vital signs that should indicate whether you suffer from depression or not. If you identify with several of the following signs and symptoms especially the first two or three, and they just won't go away, you may be suffering from depression. – Do you feel hopeless and helpless, self-loathing, strong feelings of worthlessness or guilt?

–Do you have concentration problems? – Do you have trouble focusing, making decisions, or remembering things? - You harshly criticize yourself for perceived faults and mistakes? – Have you lost interest in family, friends, activities, and things you used to enjoy? – Have you lost interest in hobbies, humour that made you smile or laugh? – Do you feel tired all the time, fatigued, sluggish, and physically drained? Your whole body may feel heavy, and even small tasks are exhausting or take longer to complete? - Has your sleep and appetite changed? - You cannot concentrate or find that previously easy tasks are now difficult. - You cannot control your negative thoughts, no matter how much you try. - Are you now much more irritable, short-tempered, feeling agitated, restless, or even violent, or aggressive than usual? – Does people get on your nerves? – Are you consuming more food, drugs, alcohol than normal, seeking false euphoria, or engaging in other reckless behaviour or engage in escapist behaviour, such as substance abuse, compulsive gambling, reckless driving, or dangerous sports? – Do you suffer from any unexplained aches and pains, an increase in physical complaints, such as headaches, back pain, aching muscles, and stomach pain? If you identify with the above, you most likely suffer from depression. Consult your doctor for advice and help. Additionally, there are experienced therapist and counsellors worldwide, to deal with depression.

Suicidal Tendencies

Most often or not, depression can lead to a major risk factor for suicide. Deep desperation, loneliness, unhappiness and hopelessness that goes along with depression can make one feel suicidal. Feeling like the only way to escape the emotional pain is to end it all. If you have a loved one who suffers from depression, take any suicidal talk or behaviour seriously and learn to recognize the warning signs. - Talking about killing or harming one's self. - Expressing strong feelings of hopelessness or being trapped. - An unusual preoccupation with death or dying. - Acting recklessly, as if they have a death wish, e.g. speeding through red lights, etc. - Calling or visiting people to say goodbye. - Getting affairs in order, giving away prized possessions, tying up loose ends. - Saying things like "Everyone would be better off without me" or "I want out". - A sudden switch from being extremely depressed to acting calm and happy. – Not caring about how they dress or looking after physical cleanness less often than before. – Not caring about their diet or physical health.

If you know somebody close to you, whose behaviour has changed dramatically, or you yourself can answer those questions, it is apparent you are feeling suicidal. Remember, you are not alone and there are many people who want to support you during this difficult time in your life. So please reach out for help! Visit your doctor or therapist and check out the Suicide Help Line or call 1-800-273- TALK in the U.S. or visit Suicide.org to find a helpline in your area or country. There are at least six percent of men and ninety-five present of women experiencing this illness. Remember, spare a moment and say a prayer for those who suffer from depression, and are suicidal. The World Health Organization predicts depression to become the second most burdensome disease ever, which means, it will cost society, in terms of medical care, sickness, days lost from work billings each year.

Low fibre diets such as fast food and processed food can tribute to depression which can lead to one being suicidal. A more healthy diet can also help keep depression under control. Not many people who suffer from depression are aware that berries and fruits work as a natural remedy to help depression.

Naturally if you do not have a healthy body, you most likely do not have a healthy mind. If your body is fatigue, so is your mind. Negative thinking can contribute to emotional depression. Low level of vitamins, iron and neutrons, such as protein can contribute to depression. Do three things each day you would normally put off. Treat yourself regularly and remember, don't forget to love yourself.

Food Additives Studies

Did you know, according to the American Institute for cancer research, we should avoid red meat, because it contains N-nitroso compounds which is associated with an increased risk of colorectal cancer. Studies have found that a large consumption of processed and red meat and saturated fats in red meat has been associated with an increased risk of type-two diabetes. Red meat itself contains certain factors that, under certain conditions, produce carcinogens salt and preservatives fats. This might explain the higher risk of heart disease, diabetes, and high blood pressure, seen with processed meats, but not with unprocessed red meats. Remember; eat healthy foods to maintain a healthier life.

Chapter Fourteen

Miracles & Testimonies

This is a beautiful poem composed by a pilgrim from Ireland, on her first visit to Medjugorje. - When I saw the church for the very first time, my heart missed a beat for our Saviour Devine, who out of love sent His Mother to this beautiful place to bring us closer together and teach us to pray. God gathers His children to shower Graces upon them as the Angels watch over on Podbrdo Hill, and when pilgrims respond to this Devine call - you can see in their faces the joy of the Lord - for the love of our dear Mother has called them here to spread the message of Medjugorje for all to hear....

Back in 2013, eleven-year-old Stephen Reilly was diagnosed with cancer. The parents of the young Irish boy claim their son was cured of terminal cancer which they believe had occurred during a pilgrimage to Medjugorje.

A young blind woman's eyesight was restored during mass in Saint Church. Many eyewitnesses experienced this Miracle, including Patrick Latta, from the house of prayer Medjugorje. He had witnessed the miracle taking place. According to Patrick and countless other eye witnesses, the blind woman had been seen, been escorted from the bus that brought them to the church. "It was easy to tell she was blind," Patrick says, "because she had a blind persons cane and was escorted from the bus into the church. Her eyesight was restored in the church. She was overwhelmed with joy when she seen colours for the very first time. She was amazed to see the statues, and the beautiful coloured flowers in the church. This miracle is recorded by the Medjugorje Parish." Patrick Latta vows. It is reported that countless people claim they were cured of cancer, brain tumours and other terminal illnesses. All miracles are recorded by the parish council of Medjugorje.

An American woman claims, after Vicka had laid hands over her, the cancerous tumour in her brain had completely vanished. Before she was to have life threatening surgery to have the tumour removed, she had an inspiration to visit Medjugorje before the operation. She claims she felt a tingling sensation inside her head where the tumour had being located. After returning to the States, and when the doctors examined her, they discovered that the tumour has completely gone. – Story account by a friend of Medjugorje.

In the summer of 2011, my son Miley who was age six at the time was going for lots of medical tests on his stomach and his digestive system. His spine is curved and was getting worse; he was in a lot of pain and also had trouble with his bowels. The doctors could not find what was causing this curvature in his spine, and his bowel problems. I heard Our Lady was appearing in Medjugorje, and there were many people who visited there on pilgrimage who claimed they were cured from physical sickness, like cancer and tumours, etc. So I decided to pack my bags and travel from my home town to Medjugorje. My intention was to pray for my son Miley, who I loved dearly. While I was there I prayed a lot for him to be cured. Then one evening at approximately six-forty, myself, my uncle and a few other pilgrims were praying the rosary at the Blue Cross. Then unexpectedly my uncle nudged me and pointed at the sun, suggesting I look at it.

Just as I looked at the sun, it immediately started to spin and change colour and it appeared to be coming closer. At the same time it was spinning. Then I noticed a man sitting on a rock across from me, he had a clock on his face. I thought this was strange, and it startled me. I had no idea what this meant. I could not see his face clearly. Then a small boy about the same age as my son, Miley, appeared out of nowhere and stood beside the man. He stood there for a couple of seconds, staring at the statue of the Blessed Mother, and then suddenly vanished into thin air. *Was this a miracle,* I asked myself. The feeling I got was that my prayers were going to be answered, and my son was going to be cured. I thanked Jesus and the Blessed Mother Mary for showing me this phenomenal experience. But the amazing thing was, two days later after arriving back home, I got my sons tests back from the hospital, and they were all normal. A Special thanks to Jesus and the Blessed Mother of Medjugorje for answering my humble prayers. Even though Miley's back is still a little curved, it has not gotten any worse. The doctors were very happy with his recovery. Even my own life has changed; I received conversion and live by the "Fruits" of Medjugorje. Thank you Jesus. – Friend of Medjugoje.

It is documented that since the beginning of the apparitions, and systematically to this present day, that millions of pilgrims who have visit Medjugorje have witnessed the sun spinning or dancing. For some pilgrims they witness this miraculous happening during the day, at different times. Yet, for most pilgrims they witness the spinning of the sun during the evening rosary, Our Lady's Apparition, and the International Mass, each evening, throughout the year. The people of Medjugorje say that the spinning of the sun has become a natural occurrence to them.

For the children who were born after the Apparitions started, they say this has been happening throughout their lives. The most peculiar thing is that there have been no reports of physical harm, or damage being caused to those pilgrims' eyes, as they watch the sun spin. Another phenomenon is the majority of people see the Holy Communion Host, spinning in the centre of the sun. Others see the sun dancing, and it moving closer and further away. Others claim they see different items around the sun, such as hearts, crosses, swords, and many colours, etc. Of course the sun does not spin, or dance in the sky. If the sun physically spun, the earth would probably quake. The spinning of the sun is one of our individual signs from God, to let us know that Our Blessed Mother is present in Medjugorje. It is reported that on August 2nd 1981, on the Feast day of Our Lady Queen of the Angels, in the late afternoon. The sun started to spin in a circle, and then it started to draw closer toward the people who witnessed this. It is recorded that there were a group of at least one-hundred-fifty people watching this miraculous occurrence.

As the entire group watched the sun spin and dance, they all witnessed figures around the sun, then it seemed to circle in the shape of a crucifix. Some wept not knowing what was happening, other went on their knees to pray. It is said that others picked up their children and ran away in fear. Then six small hearts appeared in the sky, centred around a large heart. Then a white cloud covered the Hill of Podbrdo. It took fifteen minutes for the sun to return to its normal form.

Then a week or so later, the word MIR, which means peace in Croatian, appeared written on the sky above Medjugorje. It is reported that many people witnessed this. It was on this day, during the Apparition to the visionaries that Our Lady gave Her title. That She is the Queen of Peace.

Father Jozo was a keen witness to the word written in the sky. "I remember when we saw the word MIR (peace) written in big, burning letters in the sky over the Cross on Mt. Krizevac," he recalls. "We were shocked. The moments passed, but we were unable to speak. No one dared say a word. Slowly, we came to our senses. We realized that we were still alive." This is the word of Father Jozo.

Also a local villager called Sime Dodig, states that he witnessed the word MIR written in the sky. "I left my house to go to the fountain of Jurisa for a pail of water. It was between six p.m. and six-thirty p.m. Suddenly, I saw, high in the sky, like a band of blue colour, on which were big letters. Then I was seized with great fear, *"what did this mean,"* I pondered. Two students I knew rather well were close by, Ivan Prlic and Marijana Zubac. I called out to them, saying. "Children, do you see the letters in the sky?"

"We see them, Sime" said the children in sync, with amazement, as they were in shock too, to see the letters in the sky, *what could this mean*? They mused.

"At first I was afraid. But I quickly pulled myself together. I then saw that the word MIR was written in the sky. We all knelt and we prayed in a loud voice the Our Father, Hail Mary, and Glory Be, and other prayers. I began the prayers and the children answered..." Sime Dodig recalls.

Father Janko Bubalo, a local priest, related the following information given to him by a villager named Niko Vasil. "On the second day of August, 1981, at the same time the Virgin Mary appeared to the visionaries, I was with a rather large group of people in front of the church. Suddenly, I noticed a strange play of the sun. I went to the South side of the church so as to see what was happening. First off, it seemed like a shiny wheel separated from the sun and headed toward earth. It was beautiful to see as well as frightening. The sun then began to swing back and forth. After that, some sort of shining balloons began to emerge from the sun, and that a wind pushed them about and toward Medjugorje. A lot of other people who attending the Holy Rosary, also witnessed this, and wondered *what did this mean*? Then a bundle of light, like a ray, separated itself from the sun and travelled like the rays of a rainbow, toward the place of the Holy Virgin's first appearances. It then fixed itself on the steeple of Saint James Church, upon which a clear image of the Blessed Virgin appeared, and She did not have a crown."

The following was about an event that took place on December 9th 1983. It was reported by Father Umberto Loncar, and many pilgrims, which involved the sun and Cross Mountain. "Medjugorje was a deep experience for everyone in our group." he says. "It shook us all! Mirjana received the ninth secret before our eyes in the Apparition chapel. She wept profusely. We know from Mirjana who has received all ten secrets that the ninth and tenth ones are "grave matters... a chastisement for the sins of the world...

The day after the eighth we had a sun miracle at one-pm. We had just walked behind the church in order to look up to the Cross Mountain when a storm commenced. It almost threw us over, and the church seemed to shake. Clouds, as dark as night, were driven across the sky by this brief storm. Suddenly, the sun broke through with spectacular rays and then some people saw the sun spin. All the people assembled, and got on their knees because we all saw the darting and fiery rays breaking through the dark clouds in various directions. As the clouds disappeared, the sky became rose-red and the sun paled. In the centre of the sun, was Saint Andrew Cross, and as it disappeared, a huge cross began to rise above the sun, peaked by a crown. The cross had light around it; the darkness grew again, as though the judgment of God was at hand. All the while, the cross on cross mountain was invisible. The land below and the sky around grew in darkness. Only the spectacular rose colours twirling around the illuminated Cross, raised above the sun, grew brighter and brighter. Then, it all vanished and the dreary winter day took its normal course." Testimony of Father Umberto Loncar.

Other miraculous signs connected to Medjugorje. On January 1989 at Caritas, Alabama while Marija Pavlovic-Lunetti was in America, just before the apparition of Our Lady. A sign appeared in the sky which lasted one-and-half-hours. This sign was three rainbows. Rainbows only appear on the sky when it rains. On this particular dry sunny day, one rainbow stretched from horizon to horizon. Underneath it was another upside down rainbow, inverted with its two ends connected to the rainbow stretching to the horizons. The third rainbow was a normal rainbow, with the second one touching the top of the third, upside down top. Everybody present saw the three rainbows in the sky, and many captured this on film.

Many, many pilgrims who go to Medjugorje have never climbed a mountain in their life. Somehow they are drawn to Cross Mountain and with a deep longing-desire to make the climb out of love for the Good Lord, for the sorrow of their sins, or in seeking the answer to a prayer.

The cross erected on Mount Podbrdo, where many of the apparitions had taken place, has reportedly disappeared and reappeared or else glowed as if lit with lights, although there is no electricity on the mountain. Not everyone reports seeing the same miracles at the same time. Many miraculous healings have also been reported by pilgrims which took place at Mount Podbrdo, says a friend of Medjigorje.

More of God's signs in Medjugorje. - One particular evening after the evening Mass, an American pilgrim reports to have seen a large star, and from this star came out twelve smaller stars that formed a circle. The twelve stars then formed a cross, then the letter 'M'; appeared, together with other little stars appeared to form the word 'MIR.' It lasted about five minutes.

On another occasion, after the apparition, two luminary signs in the form of rays of light were displayed on the Cross at Krizevac and on the Church. Ivan the visionary and a group of young people had been praying on Apparition Hill, and hundreds of people present saw a fire which burned without consuming anything.

On a different occasion, a shining silhouette of an Angle takes the place of the cross on mount Krizevac. People claim to have seen the sun spinning and all sorts of unexplainable signs on the top of Cross Mountain, and also on the other side of Apparition Hill. These signs have also been seen by hundreds of people from other towns for miles around Medjugorje, especially from Ljubuski. Reported by a friend of Medjugorje

When asked by the visionaries what did those signs mean? Our Lady's response was. "They are signs of God and not of natural phenomena. These are the signs of salvation; the cross is a sign of mercy, just like the heart.

The sun is the source of light, which enlightens us. - The world must find salvation while there is time. Pray with fervour. May you have the spirit of faith. All of these signs are designed to strengthen your faith until I leave you the visible and permanent sign. Also, do not be afraid; in the future, there will be signs concerning sinners, unbelievers, alcoholics, and young people. They will accept me again. The seriousness of these apparitions, and of so many supernatural signs is thus explained. It is God's way to communicate, to reach you to save man from his present course of destroying himself. Thank you for having responding to My call."

During the conflict in Bosnia, between 1991 and 1995, the Serbian military bombs were dropped over Medjugorje, and they did not go off. Other times the pilots aboard the fighter-bombers jets claim, they could not find Medjugorje, and aborted their mission which was to bomb the village. Is it reported that not one of the Medjugorje soldiers recruited in the army, died in the former Yugoslavian conflict.

This information was taken from the parish of Medjugorje's website - Throughout the first thirty years of apparitions. There were 776,320 registered priests, Bishops, Cardinals, and religious visited to Medjugorje. These are all "registered" so God only knows how many came that were unregistered. 33,569,140 communions, 532 proven and documented healings that are recorded at the parish. Close to 800 men became priests directly related to a pilgrimage to Medjugorje, and is still ongoing. Close to 200 women became nuns directly related to a pilgrimage to Medjugorje, and still ongoing. During the Youth Festival on 2015, there were 525 priests at hand and 422 for the evening prayer service and Mass. The recording of communions started in 1985, and recordings for priests started in 1986. Medjugorje cannot be approved until the apparitions cease and nobody knows when that is exactly, but these fruits cannot be denied. We also know that the church is in charge right now, and that they have completed their investigation on Medjugorje for the time being. The findings of that investigation are still in the Vatican and it is up to the Holy Father when he will announce something on Medjugorje. With all of these outward signs, just think of the countless spiritual conversions that have taken place and we are all included in those conversions. Next to the Holy Mass, the Holy Rosary is one of the most powerful prayers we have against Satan and sin. Our Lady promises many graces to those who pray the rosary. Praying the rosary is not just repeating prayers over and over again. There are four mysteries of the rosary, which we meditate upon while reciting the prayers of the rosary.

The rosary starts with the Apostles Creed, then the Our Father, the three theological virtues, faith hope and charity, and continues with the four mysteries. The Holy Rosary is - the Joyful, the Luminous, the Sorrowful, and the Glorious Mysteries. Each decade consists of the one Our Father, ten Hail of Mary's, followed by the Glory Be, after each decade.

Dear children, I call you to be my light, in order to enlighten all those who still live in darkness, to fill their hearts with Peace, and find My Son. Your shepherds need your prayers. In this special time of prayer, permit Me to transform your hearts that you may help Me to have My Son resurrect in all hearts, and that My heart may triumph. - Dear children, pray for your brothers who haven't experienced the love of God the Father, for those whose only importance is life on earth. Open your hearts towards them and see in them My Son, who loves them. Be My light and illuminate all souls where darkness reigns. As I call you to prayer for those who have not come to know the love of God, if you were to look into your hearts you would comprehend I am speaking about many of you. Thanks for having responded to My call.

When a pilgrim from the U.K. was on pilgrimage in Medjugorje, on Apparition Hill, he had taken a photograph of the statue of the Blessed Virgin. The image seems to show Our Lady's statue on fire. Naturally enough the statue was not on fire, but this is another miraculous sign that Our Lady is present.

Going back to the early days of the apparitions, a mysterious fire broke out on Mount Podbrdo, at the site of Our Lady's first apparition. In his book, "The Apparitions of Our Lady at Medjugorje", Father Svetozar Kraljevic gives an account of flames leaping on Mount Podbrdo of which Our Lady said. The fire seen by the faithful was of a supernatural character. Father Svet once wrote that a fire of unknown origin erupted on the site of the first apparition and burned for about fifteen minutes. Several hundred people saw this, including many priests and nuns. A guard, who had been stationed at the foot of the hill to prevent pilgrims from climbing to the top, later investigated the site but found no remains of the fire. Indeed, the fire had burned brightly, but consumed nothing. A sign of God, that Our Lady is present?

Message to visionary Mirjana on January second-two-thousand-sixteen, - "Dear children, as a Mother I am happy to be in the midst of you, because I would like to talk to you once again of the words of My Son and His love. I hope that you accept Me with your heart, because the words of My Son and His love are the only light and hope in the darkness of the present moment this is the only truth that you accept and you will live, you will have hearts pure and humble. My Son loves the pure and the humble. The pure hearts and humble breathe life to the words of My Son. The words of My Son and give life to those who hear it, the words of My Son is love and hope. Therefore, My dear apostles, My children, you live the words of My Son. Love yourselves as He loved you. Love each other in His name and in memory of Him. The Church is progressing and grows thanks to those who hear the words of My Son, thanks to those who love, thanks to those who suffer and suffer in silence and in the hope of the ultimate redemption. Therefore, My dear children, the words of My Son and His love are the first and the last thought of your day. Thank you! Dear children! Today also I invite you to prayer. Only by prayer and fasting can war be stopped. Therefore, my dear little children, pray and by your life, give witness that you are mine and that you belong to Me, because Satan wishes in these turbulent days to seduce as many souls as possible. Therefore, I invite you to decide for God and He will protect you and show you what you should do and which path to take. I invite all those who have said "yes" to Me to renew their consecration to My Son Jesus and His Heart, and to Me, so we can take you more intensely as instruments of peace in this un-peaceful world. Medjugorje is a sign to all of you and a call to pray and live the days of grace that God is giving you. Therefore, dear children, accept the call to prayer with seriousness. I am with you and your suffering is also mine. How many millions of times has a loving relationship with Jesus been re-ignited at Medjugorje with these beautiful words of love? I absolve you from your sins, in the name of the Father, and of the Son, and of the Holy Spirit. Thank you for having responded to My call.

My dear children, God exists and He loves you. I come to teach you how to accept that love, how to pray. I come to ask you to fast, to accept your cross each day, to accept penance, to learn to love one another by doing the things that are uncomfortable with. Thank you.

Our Mother is planning to triumph in this momentous glorious cause. Her desire is to transform all of mankind, and a spiritual transformation of entire world. Our Lady has been sent to earth by God. Her plan is to carry out Gods wishes, which is to purify the world from sin and evil, in Jesus Name. Amen.